The First Christmas

Other Books by Paul L. Maier

A Man Spoke, a World Listened

Pontius Pilate

First Easter

First Christians

The Flames of Rome

The Best of Walter A. Maier (ed.)

Josephus—The Jewish War (ed., trans. with G. Cornfeld)

Josephus—The Essential Writings (ed., trans.)

In the Fullness of Time

A Skeleton in God's Closet

Josephus—The Essential Works (ed., trans.)

Eusebius—The Church History (ed., trans.)

The True and
Unfamiliar Story

The First Christmas

PAUL L. MAIER

KREGEL PUBLICATIONS

Published by Kregel Publications, a division of Kregel, Inc., P.O. Box 2607, Grand Rapids, MI 49501. For more information about Kregel Publications, visit our Web site: www.kregel.com.

All photographs and illustrations are by the author, except for those credited in the captions.

Cover design: John M. Lucas
Interior design: Nicholas G. Richardson

ISBN 0-8254-3330-4

Printed in Hong Kong

1 2 3 4 5 / 05 04 03 02 01

Contents

Introduction

O f all religious beliefs in the world, past or present, none have more thoroughly based themselves on history than Judaism and Christianity. The divine-human encounter in the biblical faiths always involves claims about real people, living in real places, who acted in real events of the past, many of which are also cited in secular ancient history. Both testaments of the Bible use the past tense of narrative prose—history's medium—more than any other form of language.

Because Judeo-Christianity has so thoroughly influenced Western culture, we are prone to imagine that all other world religions have a similarly solid historical base. This is by no means the case. It can, in fact, be argued that *every* religious system before or since Judaism and Christianity has avoided any significant interaction with history and instead has asked its followers to believe, by sheer faith alone, the claimed revelations of its founder. This is true of the mythologies of yesterday and the cults of today, the religions of the East or the newly-crafted creeds of the West.

Whenever links with genuine history *are* claimed—as in several modern belief systems today—these are never verified by secular history or the findings of archaeology. Typically, a single founder claims divine revelation, which is subsequently written down as a holy book for his or her following. The founder may well have been historical, of course, but one looks in vain for true correlations with secular history in the founder's holy book. Rather than presenting a private, once-for-all-time revelation, Judeo-Christianity's

(*Left*) Sheep and goats grazing along the western shore of the Sea of Galilee.

7

Sculpture of "The Flight to Egypt" at the Cathedral of St. Lazarus in Autun, France. The donkey seems quite proud of its role in this journey.

Scriptures encompass a two-thousand-year-plus period—two millennia in which its holy books *constantly* interlaced themselves with history.

Instead of claiming a mythological founder, or one who materialized from the mists of the past in an appearance datable only to the nearest century or two, Christianity boldly asserts that Jesus' public ministry began (in association with that of John the Baptist) in

> . . . the fifteenth year of the reign of Tiberius Caesar, Pontius Pilate being governor of Judea, and Herod being tetrarch of Galilee, and his brother Philip tetrarch of the region of Ituraea and Trachonitis, and Lysanias tetrarch of Abilene, in the high-priesthood of Annas and Caiaphas . . . (Luke 3:1–2a RSV)

No mythological heroes or cardboard characters here! This sixfold documentation involves personalities and places, *all* of which are well known *and historical.* In fact, we know even more about this collection of proper names from sources *outside* the New Testament. The author of 2 Peter expressed Christianity's "historical advantage" splendidly: "For we did not follow cleverly devised myths . . . but we had been eyewitnesses" (1:16).

So close an intersection with history, however, could have been hazardous for Christianity. If the faith had garbled the facts of history, it would have been laid open to ridicule. But rather than seeking the shelter of unprovable traditions to avoid such risk, Christianity instead threaded its origins into the very warp and woof of the past, becoming itself part of history's fabric. For that reason, it has also been held to *much* more stringent standards of critical evaluation than any other world religious system. This, however, was the price it gladly paid for having solid historical credentials.

History, however, is not Christianity's only ally, nor is it the only avenue into the past. Its closest cousin is *archaeology*—the systematic excavation of sites whose buried artifacts deliver "hard evidence" from the past. Though the very term reflects a crusty patina of age, archaeology is a comparatively young discipline, since scientific archaeology is little more than a century old. In that short time, however, a bulging treasury of thousands of artifacts relating to the biblical world have been discovered, greatly enhancing our understanding of that world. Any interested person today can, if he or she wishes, know more about Jesus and the origins of Christianity than would have been possible for the greatest names in church history, including Calvin, Luther, Thomas Aquinas, or even Augustine.

One often hears the claim, "Nothing found by archaeologists has *ever* disagreed with biblical evidence." This is simply not true. For example, when the Hebrews fought against their enemies, foreign reports of those campaigns sometimes differed dramatically from those in the Old Testament, which is precisely what we should expect of accounts "managed" by hostile court historians. The surrounding nations never admitted their defeats and converted some, in fact, to "victories."

Nor should anyone imagine that archaeologists go off to Israel or Jordan and dig in order to prove something in the Bible. Scientific excavators dig only for the truth, letting the chips fall where they may. What is remarkable about the chips, however, is the vast percentage that fall in a manner highly congenial to the biblical record! Or, where archaeological evidence seems to conflict with Scripture, as in the excavations at Jericho, a new reading of the same evidence corrects previous misreadings.

Other useful tools for prying open the biblical past include such specialties within ancient history as the following:

Linguistics and *Literature:* Hebrew, Aramaic, and Greek studies sharpen our understanding of what the texts of the Old and New Testaments actually say, especially in the context of the other languages and literature of those times.

Geography: From the Old Testament patriarchs to St. Paul, biblical sorts always seem to be moving from one place to the next. Most of these places are identified today and can be explored.

Meteorology and *Climatology:* Are the winds, weather conditions, and famines described in Scripture credible? These specialties provide the answers.

Politics and *Law:* How can one fully understand the trial of Jesus, for example, without invoking Roman law and politics? Or the many occasions in which St. Paul faced a judge?

Economics: The Gospels are full of references to coins, taxes, tax collectors, tribute, money changers, bills, wages, and means of livelihood. Some of the very coin issues cited in Scripture have been discovered and then dated through yet another discipline: numismatics.

Sociology, botany, zoology, medicine, and other fields also have "past tenses" in the ancient world, and thus have value for biblical research. Even astronomy can play a role in helping explain the phenomenon that was the Star of Bethlehem, for example, or the darkness on Good Friday.

In dealing with the Nativity, this book will utilize all of these avenues into the past, as well as others. The wealth of information available from ancient history should, then, enrich our quest and help bridge the gap between what is secular and what is sacred in biblical antiquity.

Such an approach can yield a fourfold benefit:

1. History and its related fields give us a means by which to "check up" on the Bible, to gauge its accuracy. Those with blind faith may object that this is both faithless and unnecessary, but in view of today's critical challenges to Scripture, we have not only the right but the obligation to compare biblical evidence with secular.

2. From these different perspectives, we can see the biblical events in sharper focus and greater dimension. To use an analogy from photography, the New Testament is like the standard fifty-millimeter lens that comes with most cameras. But how gratifying it is to catch the scene from a different angle and use the telephoto or wide-angle lenses supplied by history and archaeology.

3. Problems in the biblical text can often be solved by recourse to the other ancient disciplines.

4. Gaps in the biblical record can often be filled in by correlating outside evidence from antiquity. Gaps certainly exist between the Old and New Testaments, at the close of the book of Acts, and elsewhere. In no way do these compromise the biblical record, but because Christian origins lie so conveniently in a historical plane, history can often supply appropriate data for the rest of the story.

Using both sacred and secular evidence, then, this book tells the unfamiliar story of Jesus' birth by exploring the nooks and crannies of the past for fresh information and interesting sidelights on the Nativity. Stripping away the layers of legend and folklore that nineteen centuries have imposed on the famous event, this Christmas documentary will aim to tell "how it really was" in the world of the Nativity, providing some insights that are well known, some little known, and some new.

No liberties were taken with the facts, which are documented in the Notes at the end of each chapter, most of which involve original sources.

Aerial view of Bethlehem, looking eastward over the Church of the Nativity in the upper center toward the hills of Judea. *(D. Rubinger, Israel Ministry of Tourism)*

A Caesar's Census

In those days a decree went out from Emperor Augustus that all the world should be registered. . . . All went to their own towns to be registered. Joseph also went from the town of Nazareth in Galilee to Judea, to the city of David called Bethlehem, because he was descended from the house and family of David. He went to be registered with Mary, to whom he was engaged and who was expecting a child.

—LUKE 2:1–5

The first person mentioned in Luke's familiar story of Christmas was neither Mary nor Joseph, nor shepherd nor wise man. In fact, he would seem to have had nothing at all to do with the story, for he was the Roman emperor, Caesar Augustus. And yet it was his decision, fifteen hundred miles away in Rome, that started the train of events that finally led to the birth of Jesus in Bethlehem. (Luke, more than any other New Testament author, is very careful to anchor biblical events into the secular history of his day.)

Under normal circumstances, Jesus would have been born in Nazareth, the home of Joseph and Mary. But, as Luke explains, Augustus had decreed a registration, or census, of his vast empire, and all subjects of Rome had to return for enrollment at their ancestral hometowns. Since both Joseph and Mary were distant descendants of the much-married King David, they prepared to travel down to David's city, the sleepy little town of Bethlehem in the sere and arid Judean hills, six miles southwest of Jerusalem.

Was This Trip Necessary?

That Mary ever had to endure the rigors of this eighty-mile journey on the back of a jogging donkey while in a state of very advanced pregnancy has been doubted by some scholars. Rome never required her subjects to return to their original homes for such enrollments, they claim, and Luke must have garbled his facts. But this view has been disproved by the discovery of a Roman census edict from A.D. 104 in neighboring Egypt in which taxpayers who were living elsewhere were ordered to return to their original homes for registration.[1]

The Romans required such

censuses every fourteen years. On the next page, the photograph of a papyrus fragment from the village of Bacchias in Egypt is a census declaration made in A.D. 119. It reads, in part, as follows:

To Ptolemaios, village secretary . . .

From Horos, the son of Horos, the son of Horos, his mother being Herieus, of the aforesaid village of Bacchias.

I register myself and those of my household for the house-by-house census of the past second year of Hadrian Caesar our Lord.

I am Horos, the aforesaid, a cultivator of state land, forty-eight years old, with a scar on my left eyebrow, and (I register):

my wife Tapekusis, daughter of Horos, forty-five years old, and our own child, Horos, a son, . . . years old, with no identification marks, and

Horion, another son, one year old, with no identification marks. . . .

After naming other relatives sharing their living quarters, the

Most of Israel, Jordan, and the Negev desert are visible in this photograph taken by the *Apollo 7* mission in October, 1968, with astronauts Schirra, Cunningham, and Eisele. The Sea of Galilee, half beclouded, the Jordan River, and the Dead Sea are in the left center of the picture. The Mediterranean lies at the extreme left, just above the Sinai Desert. *(NASA)*

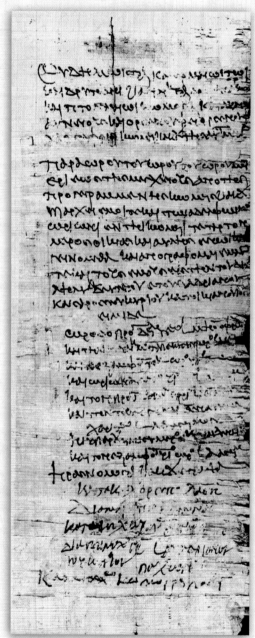

A census registration from Bacchias, Egypt, dated A.D. 119. The Greek is written in ink on papyrus. The short line at the center of the document reads "I am," followed by "Horos," etc., on the next line. (*U. of Michigan*)

document is signed by the village registrar and three official witnesses.[2]

An obscure Galilean couple had to obey a distant Caesar because sixty years earlier the Roman general Pompey had conquered Palestine, and the land had been forced into the Roman universe. Currently, it was under Rome's control as a "client kingdom" ruled by a local king, Herod the Great, who was directly responsible to the Roman emperor.

Augustus himself, the grand-nephew and adopted heir of Julius Caesar, was Rome's first emperor. His fascinating career began in the bloody civil wars of the late Roman republic, continued beyond a victorious showdown with his archrival Mark Antony, and culminated in a lengthy era of peace and prosperity, well named the *Pax Augusta*—for Augustus created and preserved the happy concord throughout the forty-four years of his rule.

Less familiar than the vaunted glories of Augustus' reign—the conquered lands and kings, or the Rome he transformed from brick into marble—is the man's intriguing religious policy. Had he not been emperor, Caesar Augustus might well have gone down in history as a religious reformer, for he tried to revive the drooping interest in Rome's state religion. By his day the average Roman had abandoned any belief in the gods of Greco-Roman mythology, and philosophical skepticism was growing, while the more credulous joined the foreign mystery cults that had invaded the empire. Augustus, however, felt that this neglect of the gods was demoralizing Roman society and that only a full restoration of the old republican piety would preserve its greatness.

So, he set about his religious revival with enthusiasm. He fairly rained temples and shrines down on the empire, restoring eighty-two temples in the city of Rome alone. He became *pontifex maximus* ("highest priest") in the state cult and tried to spark a moral renewal in society.

Too Many Bachelors

Many Roman men and women of the time were indulging in a very easy morality to escape what they called "the tedium of marriage," and soon marital and birth rates had dwindled alarmingly. One day, Augustus was disturbed enough to stalk into the Forum and devise a crude test of the situation: he told a crowd of men gathered there to separate into two groups, the bachelors on one side, the married men on the other. The handful of husbands was so much smaller that he launched into an anguished harangue against the bachelors that began, classically:

What shall I call you? *Men?* But you aren't fulfilling the duties of men. *Citizens?* But for all your efforts, the city is perishing. *Romans?* But you are in the process of blotting out this name altogether! . . . What humanity would be left if all the rest of mankind should do what you are doing? . . . *You are committing murder* in not fathering in the first place those who ought to be your descendants![3]

. . . and on to other such gems of imperial logic.

Augustus followed this bluster with legislation designed to reverse the tide by making promiscuity a crime, while conferring political advantages on a father of three children. Bachelors who shirked "the duty of marriage" were penalized in their right to inherit, and they could not even secure good seats at the games! The bachelors, of course, tried to circumvent such penalties by "marrying" infant girls, but Augustus quickly countered by setting the minimum age for engagement at ten for girls, with a two-year upper limit for length of courtship.

Perhaps it was to gauge his success in raising the marriage and birth rates that Augustus was so concerned about the imperial census, and he took several, as in the Christmas story, during his lengthy reign. Such enrollments, of course, were also the basis for the Roman system of taxation. Later census returns showed a considerable increase in

Statue of Augustus as commander-in-chief (about 20 B.C.), addressing his troops. The symbols on the breastplate indicate Augustus' achievements of prosperity and peace for the Empire (*Vatican Museum*).

When Jesus was born, the entire Mediterranean world was governed from Rome. The ruins of her ancient Forum still stand.

the population, though this may have been due as much to the return of peace and prosperity after all the bloodshed of Rome's civil wars as to Augustus' legislation. But the emperor was pleased enough with the results that he proudly mentioned his censuses in eighth place among the thirty-five "Acts of Augustus" for which he wished to be remembered, items that were later engraved on two bronze plaques outside his mausoleum.

Unfortunately, he reported figures only for that privileged group in the empire known as male Roman citizens:

The census of
   28 B.C. showed 4,063,000 citizens
   8 B.C. showed 4,233,000 citizens
   A.D. 14 showed 4,937,000 citizens

At this time, however, the entire Roman Empire—like Luke, the Romans also hyperbolized it as "the whole world"—would have numbered almost 55,000,000 people.

The census mentioned in the Nativity account was a provincial enrollment possibly associated with the citizens' census of 8 B.C., but apparently the machinery necessary to take it in far-off Palestine was not prepared until about 5 B.C., since 8 B.C. is some three years too early for the birth of Christ. (For reasons that will be explained in a later chapter, we know that Jesus was *not* born in A.D. 1.)

An Unknown Subject

One might wonder how Augustus would have reacted to this Judean census in which—had he chosen to examine the returns from Bethlehem—the following group of three names would have been included:

Yoseph Ben-Iacob, carpenter
Mariam Bath-Ioachim, his wife
Yeshua [Jesus], first-born son[4]

Did Augustus ever even see the names? The chances are virtually nil. Certainly, he never learned the significance of what had happened

(*Right*) The mausoleum of Augustus near the Tiber River at the northern edge of ancient Rome.

in Bethlehem because of his decision to take the census.

At the time of Augustus' death in A.D. 14, Jesus was about nineteen years old, an apprentice carpenter in Nazareth, and the emperor still could not possibly have heard of him. He would have been astounded to know that later ages would assign his own death to the year A.D. 14 ("in the year of the Lord") rather than the Roman date, 767 A.U.C. *(ab urbe condita,* "from the founding of the city"), all because of that unknown subject, born in Bethlehem. And he would have been amazed that future generations would wish one another a "Merry Christmas" rather than *"Io Saturnalia!"*—that great end-of-the-year festival in Rome that featured pagan delights and many of the holiday trappings of our secular yuletide, including holly, mistletoe, evergreens, the exchange of gifts, and much feasting and drinking.

But the successors of the emperor and of the baby would discover one another soon enough.

Endnotes

1. Roman census edict in Egypt: This decree, from A.D. 104, begins, "Gaius Vibius Maximus, prefect of Egypt, says: The house-to-house census having started, it is essential that all persons who for any reason whatsoever are absent from their homes be summoned to return to their own hearths, in order that they may perform the customary business of registration. . . ." See A. H. M. Jones, ed., *A History of Rome Through the Fifth Century* (New York: Harper & Row, 1970), II, 256f.

2. Census declaration from Bacchias, Egypt: See J. G. Winter, ed., *Papyri in the University of Michigan Collection,* III (Ann Arbor: Univ. of Michigan Press, 1936), 185–87.

3. Augustus: The harangue against the bachelors is recorded by Dio Cassius, *Roman History* (hereafter merely "Dio Cassius") 1vi, 1–10. The "Acts of Augustus," recording his census, are *Res Gestae Divi Augusti* 8. For the emperor's career, see Suetonius, *Augustus;* Dio Cassius, 1i–1vi; Velleius Paterculus, *Compendium* ii, 84–124.

4. Yosef Ben-Iacob, etc.: These reconstructions of their names mean "Joseph, son of Jacob" and "Mary, daughter of Joachim." For the identities of these fathers, see notes to chapters 10 and 11.

(Right) The ruins of the ancient Roman Forum still stand amid the modern city. To the left are the columns of the Temple of Castor and Pollux, at left center is the Arch of Septimus Severus, and at right center, the squarish, reconstructed Senate House.

Palestine the Paradox

Now the Lord said to Abram, "Go from your country . . . to the land that I will show you. I will make of you a great nation. . . . To your offspring I will give this land."

—GENESIS 12:1, 2, 7

Palestine is a land rippling with irony. It gave birth to two great religions and nurtured a third, yet it may be the most bitterly contested spot on earth. Jews, Christians, and Muslims all call it the Holy Land, but probably more blood has been spilled there per acre than anywhere else in the world. The ancient Hebrews claimed it as their Promised Land because of the divine pledge to Abraham, and yet they had to fight the Philistines to win it. And then they saw it crushed by invading Assyrians and Babylonians, mauled by Egyptians, torn by Syrians, and finally conquered by Romans.

But this is merely the record up to the time of the first Christmas, when the baby called "The Prince of Peace" was born. After that, the land was assaulted by the Persians, Arabs, Crusaders, Mamelukes, Turks, and British, while today it smolders with Arab-Israeli hostilities.

Why this sickening saga of bloodshed? One prime reason is because the three major faiths of Western civilization regard Palestine as their own religious cradle, and each, at one time or another, has taken up arms against the other two "strangers in the nursery." To Jews, it is the land of the sacred Torah; to Christians, that of the Old and New Testaments; and to Muslims, it is Abraham's country—they also claim him as patriarch through his son Ishmael—while Jerusalem marks the spot, so they teach, where Muhammed's steed last touched earth before ascending into heaven with the prophet on his back.[1]

But blame for the bloodshed must also be deposited squarely at the doors of geography and politics. Palestine has the glory of being located at the juncture of two continents—Africa and Asia—and so served as the crossroads of antiquity. But this strategic location also proved a heavy burden. The armies of the ancient world, even if they had no quarrel with the people of Palestine, regularly used the land as a causeway en route to attacking one another, ravaging Palestine in the process. The inhabitants had as much safety as would a flock of sparrows that chose to build their nests on a superhighway.

Overrun, despoiled, devastated, and small (roughly the size and shape of Vermont twisted upside down), Palestine still exerted probably the most powerful influence on subsequent civilization, per capita, of any land in history. Its Hebrew inhabitants gave the world monotheism and a system of ethics that has not been superseded—which law on any of the nations' lawbooks is not a corollary of one of the Ten Commandments?— and its Christians seeded a faith that is believed by two billion people today. It has been rightly said that Western civilization is like a family whose mother was Hebrew, whose father was Greek, and that moved away to live in Rome.

A Geographic Marvel

Even if it had no religious significance, Palestine would be an intriguing land. In fact, it is an earth scientist's paradise, boasting a Sea of Galilee that is almost 700 feet *below* sea level and a wriggling stream called the Jordan that channels Galilee's fresh water and empties it into an oblong, finger-shaped basin of brackish fluid known as the Dead Sea. Jordan means *descender,* an appropriate name for its own 600-foot drop, and yet it is hardly a straight gorge, for it twists and loops some 200 miles to make the 65-mile trip from Galilee to the Dead Sea as the crow flies.

The Dead Sea is 1,286 feet below sea level, and if some mad engineer were to cut a canal up to the Mediterranean, the whole Jordan valley would soon be overwhelmed with a quivering mass of water a quarter-mile high. The Dead Sea basin is, quite literally, the lowest place in the world—six times as far below sea level as Death Valley in California. (The lowest spot on the earth's crust is the sea bottom within the Marianas

The Jordan River as it emerges from the Sea of Galilee. The Golan Heights are in the background.

21

trench in the Pacific Ocean, where soundings have reached an ocean depth of more than 36,000 feet.) At least 25 percent salt and other minerals—compared with 5 percent for the ocean—the Dead Sea is so dense that a swimmer can barely submerge in it and is flipped to the surface like a cork. Fish leaving the Jordan delta waters die within minutes after swimming into the Dead Sea, and the evaporation rate is so fierce that it equals or exceeds the incoming flow of the Jordan.

Even the underground regions here rumble with a separate fascination of their own. Underlying the whole depression are subterranean gases and volcanic activity that bubble up hot springs and asphalt, and periodically cause earthquakes. These phenomena may well have been responsible for the fall of those famed sin capitals in Old Testament times, Sodom and Gomorrah.[2]

More than anything else, Palestine resembles an accordion-fold of land,

with four diverse bands running north and south. Bordering the Mediterranean to the west is a flat and fertile coastal plain; next to it rises a central hilly plateau on which Jerusalem and Bethlehem are located; beyond that plunges the Great Rift valley of the Jordan and the Dead Sea; and finally the tablelands of the Transjordan rise abruptly to the east.

But political lines directly crisscrossed this geography at the time of the birth of Christ, dividing the land into three bands running east and west: rolling, verdant Galilee to the north, the picturesque home of Joseph and Mary; Samaria in the center, the bleached land of those despised half-breed cousins of the Jews called the Samaritans; and Judea to the south, the more barren and hilly religious and political center of the land. Because of their trip down to Bethlehem, the subsequent flight to Egypt, and their eventual return to Nazareth, the Holy Family would traverse the greater part of Palestine before the Christmas story reached its conclusion.

(Left) The Sea of Galilee, looking northwest toward Tarichaeae (Magdala).

A White Christmas?

What kind of weather they would have encountered has evoked the widest range of guesses. Old sixteenth-century European woodcuts show Joseph and Mary all bundled up, braving the blizzards of a north German winter on the way to Bethlehem. The humorous thought of a snowstorm in a subtropical climate aside, it is by no means certain that the Nativity even took place in the winter months.

But, assuming for the moment that it did, *could* the first Christmas have been a white one? This is highly improbable, certainly, but by no means impossible, as many insist. Snow does fall in the Jerusalem area about three or four days each winter and sometimes in considerable quantity: in January 1950, twenty inches fell; in February 1920, twenty-nine inches. The meteorology, then, would allow a very remote possibility of snow at Bethlehem on that day that would shift history.

Palestine lies between 31 and 33 degrees north latitude, in the same parallel as Georgia, Arizona, Nagasaki, and Shanghai. But since it is adjacent to that great climatic storage battery called the Mediterranean Sea, its weather is moderate and two-seasonal: a cool but not uncomfortable winter, when some rain falls; and a summer in which the sun often shines 98 percent of the daytime.

However, because of the wide variety in the forms and altitude of its tortured terrain—ranging from 9,230-foot Mt. Hermon in the north to the Dead Sea depression in the south, from fertile vales to blazing deserts—local climates in Palestine can vary from subarctic to torrid. Some have even suggested that one reason the Bible is intelligible nearly everywhere in the world is that Palestine offers a bit of almost all the geographic and climatic conditions on earth. At least there is reason enough for the pictorial variety offered on Christmas cards displaying backgrounds from the Holy Land that seem to clash.

Endnotes
1. Muhammed's trip to Jerusalem: *Sura* xvii, 1ff. in the Qu'ran.
2. Dead Sea area: The Hebrews called it the Salt Sea; the Greeks, the Asphalt Lake. See Strabo, *Geographica* xvi, 2, 42. The destruction of Sodom and Gomorrah is related in Genesis 19.

(Right) The Sea of Galilee at sunrise over the Golan Heights.

A Galilean Couple

Now the birth of Jesus the Messiah took place in this way. When his mother Mary had been engaged to Joseph, but before they lived together, she was found to be with child from the Holy Spirit.

—MATTHEW 1:18

Nazareth is usually the forgotten town in the Christmas story, but this is where it all began. The Galilean village was indeed a very forgettable place in ancient times. Astonishingly, there is no mention of Nazareth in the Old Testament or the Talmud, and later on one of Jesus' future disciples would sneer, "Can anything good come out of Nazareth?" (John 1:46).

"Indeed!" the world has since replied, not only because of the awesome figure of Jesus but also because of the very beautiful story of his origin. Nestled in one of the hills of lower Galilee overlooking the triangular Plain of Esdraelon,

Nazareth was an insignificant village far smaller than the present bustling city of fifty-seven thousand. Its secluded inhabitants had to travel northward over four miles of back roads to get to Sepphoris in order to purchase the many items not available in Nazareth.

This is where Joseph would buy whatever carpenter's tools and supplies he had not inherited from his father. The Gospels tell us very little about Joseph, but if he resembled the pious, hard-working class of his Jewish colleagues in Galilee, he would not think of marriage until he was at least twenty-five years old. In contrast, it was customary for girls to marry shortly after puberty, and how this young craftsman became engaged to a fifteen- or sixteen-year-old girl named Mary is not recorded. Certainly they must sometime have met at one of the harvest festivals, if not at the village well in Nazareth—it was the sole source of water supply—and in a hamlet the size of Nazareth, everyone knew everyone else.

Their Ancestry

"Yosef" and "Miriam," as pronounced in their own languages, were common names among the Jews of that day. While these two do not show up in secular history, both Matthew and Luke carefully give Jesus' genealogy through Joseph (Matt. 1:1ff.; Luke 3:23ff.). It is no secret, however, that these two genealogies do *not* fully agree, a fact embarrassing to some Christians and gleefully used by critics in trying to undermine the historicity of the Nativity.

But this is no recent problem newly discovered by scoffers! The issue is merely 1,800 years old, and no one has given it a better solution than Eusebius in his *Church History*, who quotes the Christian scholar Julius Africanus (early A.D. 200s) as follows:

> Names in the families of Israel were reckoned either according to nature [physical parentage] or law; by nature in the case of genuine offspring; by law when another man fa-

thered children in the name of a brother who had died childless.[1]

Matthew's genealogy records the natural, biological ancestry of Joseph, and Luke the legal ancestry, according to Deuteronomy 25:5–6. We would, of course, have preferred that both genealogies had focused instead on Mary, but in the patriarchal society of the time, genealogies were always traced through the male line. Since the Israelites were not to intermarry, according to Mosaic law, Mary also had Davidic ancestry, and thus the genealogies would also apply to her.

The Engagement

Romance and courtship did not play a large role in ancient times, and most marriages were arranged between the parents of the couple. However, bride and groom were not simply thrown at each other in a loveless match. Directly or indirectly, their comments and conduct often alerted parents as to which family to contact, and love was indeed a factor in many of the alliances.

Nazareth, overlooking the Church of the Annunciation, which was built over the presumed site where Mary was greeted by the angel.

"The Annunciation" by Fra Angelico, painted c. 1433 for San Domenico in Cortona, Italy. (*Museo Diocesano, Cortona*)

What most probably happened was this. One day, Joseph asked his parents if he could marry that village girl who was his distant relative, Mary. They discussed it among themselves before giving him an answer, carefully appraising Mary's parentage, ancestry, and resources. The last, of course, was not a prime consideration, since everyone in Nazareth was poor. And they could hardly fault Mary's background, for it was the same as their own: although humble, both families were distant descendants of the royal family of Israel, and they could proudly trace their family tree back to King David and one of his many wives. They easily approved Joseph's choice, probably with enthusiasm.

Then Joseph's father paid a call to Mary's parents, who would act duly surprised as the purpose of the visit grew plain. But Mary's random comments about the young carpenter Joseph had all but shouted her interest, and so the discussion began in earnest, the two fathers doing most of the negotiating. In biblical times, marriage was considered a covenant between two families, not just the bridal pair, so there were many matters to discuss besides the dowry, which would have been small in any case.

Finally, the fathers agreed to a marriage contract between their children. Joseph was then brought before Mary, and their parents uttered a formal benediction over them as they tasted a cup of wine together. This, the legal betrothal, was far more binding than the modern engagement. Only divorce could break it, and even though they were not yet married, had either Joseph or Mary been unfaithful to the other, it would have been deemed an adultery punishable by death.[2] Had Joseph died in the meantime, Mary would have been his legal widow.

Since betrothal was nearly tantamount to marriage, could the couple enjoy lawful sexual relations? There is some evidence that engaged Judean couples could and did exercise this privilege, even though

(*Right*) Greek Orthodox Church of St. Gabriel in Nazareth, built over the well where an early tradition claims that Mary was greeted by the angel.

both still lived at home with their parents. In the more conservative Galilean countryside, however, virginity was maintained until the wedding itself, which laid great stress on prior purity. In the case of Joseph and Mary, the New Testament is explicit in stating that Joseph did not know Mary sexually until after the birth of Jesus (Matt. 1:24f.).

The Annunciation

One day, during the months between her engagement and marriage, Mary's wedding preparations were momentously interrupted. Luke tells the familiar story of the angel Gabriel appearing to Mary with the words, "Greetings, favored one! The Lord is with you! . . . And now, you will conceive in your womb and bear a son, and you will name him Jesus. He will be great, and will be called the Son of the Most High . . . and of his kingdom there will be no end" (Luke 1:28, 31–33).

One reason many moderns doubt the story, quite apart from the angel, is that any such apparition should have frightened the poor girl out of her wits. And yet Mary was brought up immediately after Old Testament times, in which, her elders reported, angelic visits were commonplace. So her immediate reaction was quite logical indeed: "How can this be, since I am a virgin?"

"The Holy Spirit will come upon you," Luke records the angel's reply, "and the power of the Most High will overshadow you; therefore the child to be born will be holy; he will be called Son of God" (Luke 1:35).

Mary agreed in simple trust. "Here am I, the servant of the Lord; let it be with me according to your word" (Luke 1:38).

Under the assumption that it must have taken even a divine-human baby the normal term to develop, Christendom appointed March 25 (exactly nine months before December 25) as the Feast of the Annunciation, when Jesus was conceived. The emphasis, however, is not on any calendar precision—the exact date of the Nativity is unknown—but on the commemoration itself.

For Mary, the news that she would bear the long-awaited Messiah who

30

had been promised her people was both joyful and staggering. It filled her with a sense of wonder to which she finally gave expression in the Magnificat, spoken at the home of her cousin Elizabeth, mother of John the Baptist, whom she visited shortly after the Annunciation. Her exultant words began, "My soul magnifies the Lord, and my spirit rejoices in God my Savior. . . ." and they would become part of the Christian liturgy (Luke 1:46ff.).

But Mary's pregnancy was cruel and shocking news to Joseph, for he knew that he was not the father. Probably he could not really believe Mary's story of the angelic visit, so he had to agonize over a decision based on three options: (1) marry the girl quickly and hope the tongues in Nazareth would someday stop wagging over a six-month baby; (2) publicly divorce Mary as an adulteress, in which case she would be stoned to death; or (3) have the marriage contract set aside quietly, while Mary went off to have her baby elsewhere.

Being a good and pious sort, Joseph would not marry an adulter-ess, but he loved Mary too much to wish her public shame and death. So he quickly decided on the third alternative. But then, as Matthew recorded it, there was another angelic interposition in the Nativity story:

> An angel of the Lord appeared to him in a dream and said, "Joseph, son of David, do not be afraid to take Mary as your wife, for the child conceived in her is from the Holy Spirit. She will bear a son, and you are to name him Jesus, for he will save his people from their sins." (Matthew 1:20–21)

How easily Mary's story jibed after such an experience! Now sharing his betrothed's incredible secret, Joseph could bury his suspicions and anxieties, and marry his beloved as soon as possible.

The Marriage

Probably no more than a week or two afterward, the wedding was celebrated in Nazareth. From various clues scattered across Scripture, it

Mary's Well in Nazareth, a natural spring that has flowed for centuries and may well have been the place where Mary drew water for her household. Today it is sheltered inside the apse of the Greek Orthodox Church of St. Gabriel in Nazareth.

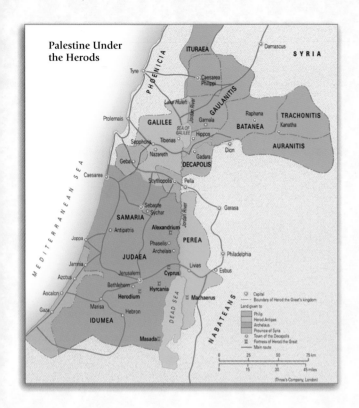

Palestine Under the Herods

(Three's Company, London)

seems that biblical nuptials were more similar to modern weddings than different from them. The two bridal parties marched in procession, accompanied by music, to the place where they would be married, the bride and groom wearing garlands and jewelry, and the bride a veil, too. There were attendants on both sides, and a wedding feast followed, which could be quite elaborate. Samson's nuptial banquet lasted for seven days (Judg. 14:12), but such affairs in Nazareth were always on a smaller scale.[3]

For the next five months, Mary lived happily at Joseph's house, her pregnancy now obvious. One day came news of the Roman emperor's edict requiring all of his subjects to enroll themselves for the census at their ancestral homes. However much they must have dreaded the prospect of a five- or six-day trip down to Bethlehem when Mary was in advanced pregnancy, Joseph and Mary quickly realized that Augustus' decree very nicely solved two formidable problems for them. They could never go to Bethlehem and return again before Jesus' birth, so he

would now have to be born in Judea, and any prying neighbors in Nazareth need never know that theirs was apparently a six-month baby. At this stage, it would have been useless to try to explain to them the wonderful kind of child this really was.

The other difficulty concerned the familiar prophecy that the Messiah was to be born in Bethlehem. In fact, it was the only cloud smudging Mary's happiness, for if she were intended to bear the Christ, why had God chosen a girl living in Nazareth rather than in Bethlehem? The news from Rome easily placed the last piece of the divine-human puzzle into place. Even though Joseph could probably have attended to the census obligations in Bethlehem alone, Mary had every reason to make the trip also.

Commending their few valuables to his father's keeping, Joseph and Mary gathered their necessities and set out for Bethlehem. The picture of Joseph tenderly guiding the donkey on which Mary was sitting—a little apprehensive lest the birth pangs come too early—is so enshrined in imagination, art, and literature that it needs no further comment.

What route they chose for the trip south is not so graphic or definite. It could well have been the central route via the valleys winding through the hills of Samaria, which was the shortest. However, if the pious Joseph wanted to avoid any contact with the Samaritans or wished to keep Mary warm during a chilly time of the year, he could have chosen an alternate route southeast across the Plain of Esdraelon, down the Jordan River valley as far as Jericho, and then up to Jerusalem and Bethlehem.

In either case, Mary would suffer discomforts on this eighty- or ninety-mile journey—the legends that she was miraculously spared them are all apocryphal—but she would soon forget the pain in joy at the extraordinary thing about to happen to her. The birth of any child is a marvel of its own, but that of a divine child, as she believed hers to be, was an incalculable wonder.

The Jordan River, near the place where Jesus was baptized.

Endnotes

1. Differences in genealogies: Eusebius, *The Church History* 1.7.
2. Death penalty for adultery with betrothed: According to Deuteronomy 22:23, "If there is a young woman, a virgin already engaged to be married, and a man meets her in the town and lies with her, you shall bring both of them to the gate of that town and stone them to death. . . ."
3. Marriage customs: References to engagement and marriage in biblical times are scattered widely across the Old and New Testaments. Extracanonical sources are I Maccabees 9:39; Tobit, and elsewhere.

An Undatable Date

But when the fullness of time had come, God sent his Son, born of woman, born under the law, in order to redeem those who were under the law, so that we might receive adoption as children.

—*GALATIANS 4:4–5*

Paul's famous comment that the Nativity happened "in the fullness of time" is usually interpreted to mean that God had a good sense of timing, since conditions prevailing in the Mediterranean world could not have been more favorable for the spread of Christianity. The Old Testament had predicted the birth of a Messiah for centuries, and the Greeks had given their world a universal language through which Jesus' message could spread easily and quickly. The Roman Empire had organized the whole Mediterranean basin into one vast communications network, almost perfectly geared to foster the spread of Christianity, since its missionaries could travel from city to city without fear of piracy at sea or brigands by land. Rome had also spread the welcome blanket of peace across the world, the *Pax Romana*, a time in which the new faith could thrive.

And so the first Christmas happened "in the fullness of time" indeed. But precisely *when* was that time? Unfortunately, there is no exact answer. Ironically, the event that has divided our reckoning of time into years B.C. and A.D., is itself almost undatable. "Everyone knows" Jesus must have been born on December 25, A.D. 1, but it is not quite that simple, and certainly this date is wrong. For Herod the Great died in the spring of 4 B.C., and the king was very much alive during the visit of the Magi in the Christmas story.[1] Therefore, Jesus would have to have been born before this time, and his birth is usually set during the winter of 5–4 B.C. ("Before Christ," or, incredibly "Before Himself").[2]

(Right) Panorama of modern Jerusalem from the Mount of Olives. In the foreground is the Kidron Valley. To the right stands the Dome of the Rock, where the temple was situated. To the left and rear of this, a white spire marks the approximate location of Golgotha.

Why then, is our calendar four or five years off? Why is the present decade not 2000–2010 but, literally A.D. 2005–2015 *(anno Domini, "in the year of the Lord")*?

It was a sixth-century Roman monk-mathematician-astronomer named Dionysius Exiguus (Dionysius the Little) who unknowingly committed what became history's greatest numerical error in terms of cumulative effect. For in reforming the calendar to pivot about the birth of Christ, he dated the Nativity in the year 753 from the founding of Rome, when in fact Herod had died only 749 years after Rome's founding. The result of Dionysius' chronology, which remains current, was to give the correct traditional date for the founding of Rome, but one that is at least four or five years off for the birth of Christ.

While Jesus may have been born as early as 7 B.C., such earlier datings for the Nativity would make him a little too old for the "about thirty years" of age when he began his public ministry in A.D. 28–29 (Luke 3:23). Unfortunately, it is not pos-sible to work back to an exact date for Jesus' birth from any later information about his adult life.[3]

The Season?

But surely the New Testament provides other chronological clues. Luke tried to date the event with some precision in his famous prologue about Augustus' decree "that all the world should be registered. This was the first registration and was taken while Quirinius was governor of Syria" (2:1–2). The solution, then, is merely to find the date for Augustus' imperial census, as well as the dates for the Syrian governor Quirinius's term in office.

And how scholars have tried to do just that—and with what little success! The imperial citizens' census of 8 B.C., discussed in the first chapter, reached Palestine as a broadened provincial census anytime between that year and perhaps 6 or 5 B.C., as indicated, a range too broad for much help in pinpointing the time of the first Christmas.

But the governor of Syria, Publius Sulpicius Quirinius, is known from

Roman records. He had been a consul, with military and business successes to his credit, though a chronic avarice stained his memory. But when was he governor of Syria? Not until A.D. 6–7, according to ancient records, which is eleven years too late for the Nativity census, and Luke has been faulted for inaccuracy here. Elsewhere, however, Luke is extremely careful in naming Greek and Roman officials, and since a similar provincial census in Gaul required forty *years* to complete, Luke may have been referring to a preliminary enrollment in Herod's Judea, during which census data was collected and then used later for the actual assessment of taxes under Quirinius in A.D. 6. Some scholars, therefore, suggest an alternate reading of Luke's text: "This census was first really carried out when Quirinius was governor of Syria," i.e., a decade later. The Greek syntax here can also be translated: "This enrollment was *before* that made when Quirinius was governor of Syria." In any case, Quirinius helps very little in any dating of the Nativity.[4]

What about the great Star of Bethlehem that attracted the Wise Men? Astral events are indeed prime props in any chronology, but astronomers have never agreed on exactly what the star may have been, so it is difficult to date it. (Nevertheless, the Star of Bethlehem is so fascinating a phenomenon in its own right that it will be discussed in a later chapter.)

Adding up all the clues, hints, and shreds of evidence from every available source, many scholars set the date for the Nativity sometime in the fall of 5 B.C. Others maintain it must have happened in spring, because the shepherds were out in the fields, "keeping watch over their flock by night" (Luke 2:8), at the angelic announcement, which would suggest lambing time. Only then, presumably, did shepherds bother to guard their flocks at night. In the winter, sheep would have been in the corral.

This clue seems impressive enough, but it is by no means conclusive. In many of the rural districts of Palestine, the flocks were not fed in pens but had to forage for their food in both summer and winter. During the great winter snowfall of 1910–11 in Syria, hundreds of thousands of sheep died because snow covered the ground for weeks, interrupting their feeding. And a passage in the Jewish *Mishnah* states that some sheep pastured near Bethlehem were destined for sacrifice at the temple in Jerusalem and suggests that these flocks lay out in the fields all year around.[5]

Since shepherding seems to be one of the least changed occupations in Palestine over the last two thousand years, it may be instructive to gauge the present practice. The famed Chautauqua and Lyceum lecturer, Stephen A. Haboush, the former "Shepherd Boy of Galilee," writes:

> As a boy, I kept our flock through the fall of the year and up to the first of January out among the low hills and valleys around the Sea of Galilee. But during the rainy season in January and February, I would keep the sheep in the fold back of our home in Tiberias. In Judea, however, where there is only half as much annual rainfall, the shepherds keep their flocks grazing out in the valleys for most of the months of the winter season, as I know from members of my tribe.[6]

And Christmastime visitors to Bethlehem today tell of seeing shepherds out in the fields with their sheep, their heads muffled against the chilly weather in colorful *keffiyehs.*

The Day?

Why is Christmas celebrated on December 25? The early Christian church seems to have observed the birth of Christ on January 6 in the East and on December 25 in the West, but both practices began too late—the A.D. 300s—to warrant attaching any precision to these dates. Probably, it was a matter of substitution. The Romans of the time not only celebrated their Saturnalia festival at the close of December but they also thought that December 25 marked the date of the winter solstice (instead of December 21), when they observed the pagan feast of *Sol Invictus,* the Unconquerable Sun, which was just in the act of turning about to aim northward once again. Christianity sought to replace these pagan festivals with a Christian celebration honoring the "sun of righteousness," a common epithet for Jesus as Messiah. Yet Christmas, even with its Christian name, has never been able to shake off the secular roots of this end-of-the-year festival. But all this should not obscure the fact that, according to the best reckoning, Jesus may indeed have been born in the fall or winter of 5 B.C.

One could wish that an event of this importance were more precisely datable. Yet the ancients, especially in the Near East, had a less exacting view of time than did later ages with their accurate clocks and calendars. At a period when there was no universal system of chronology, and events were dated "in the reign of King [Such and Such]" or "in the governorship of [So and So]," when numbers were often rounded off, and even the methods of counting years differed, perhaps it is fortunate we can come within months of the actual date of the first Christmas. But the final paradox, certainly, is that something as imprecisely datable as the birth of Christ later served as the technical anchor date for the calendar used almost everywhere in the world today, which we find quite precise indeed.

Time, however, had a wholly different meaning for the pair just finishing that uncomfortable journey down to Bethlehem. The question nagging at Joseph and Mary as they threaded their way through that florid symphony of noise and color that was Jerusalem was this: Would they reach Bethlehem in time for the event that now seemed imminent?

Endnotes

1. Death of Herod: The English scholar W. E. Filmer has suggested that Herod may have died as late as 1 B.C., but this alternate chronology has not been generally accepted, since it is too difficult to reconcile with the regnal dates of Herod's sons and successors. It seems that Herod did indeed die in 4 B.C. For further detail on the chronology of Christmas, see the admirable study by Professor Jack Finegan, *Handbook of Biblical Chronology*, 215ff.
2. Death of Herod: The chronology is discussed by Finegan, *Biblical Chronology* (Princeton, 1964), 230ff. See also W. E. Filmer, "The Chronology of the Reign of Herod the Great," *The Journal of Theological Studies* (hereafter *JTS*), XVII (October 1966), 283–98. An excellent response to Filmer is P. M. Bernegger, "Affirmation of Herod's Death in 4 B.C.," *JTS*, XXXIV (1983), 526–31; and Harold W. Hoehner, "The Date of the Death of Herod the Great" in J. Vardaman and E. M. Yamauchi, eds., *Chronos, Kairos, Christos* (Winona Lake, IN: Eisenbrauns, 1989), 101–11.
3. Chronology of Jesus' life: See Finegan, *Biblical Chronology*, 215ff.; Paul L. Maier, "Sejanus, Pilate, and the Date of the Crucifixion," *Church History*, XXXVII (March 1968), 1–11; and Maier, "The Date of the Nativity and the Chronology of Jesus' Life" in Vardaman, *Chronos*, 113–30.
4. Quirinius: Tacitus, *Annals* ii; 30; iii, 22, 23, 48; Suetonius, *Tiberius* x1ix; Dio Cassius 1iv, 48; Josephus, *Antiquities* 17:355; 18:1, 26; 20:102. For Quirinius and the census, see also *Corpus inscriptionum Latinarum*, III, Suppl. 6687; Lily R. Taylor, "Quirinius and the Census of Judaea," *The American Journal of Philology*, 54 (1933), 120–33; Finegan, *Biblical Chronology*, 234–38; and A. N. Sherwin-White, *Roman Society and Roman Law in the New Testament* (Oxford: Clarendon, 1963); 162–71. The last calls a provincial census of Judea during the reign of Herod the Great "an impossibility" (p. 163), but Herod, as client-king, might easily have cooperated with Augustus' well-known proclivities for censuses in the provinces. See Tactitus, *Annals* vi, 41.
5. Sheep in the fields most of the year: The *Mishnah* has differing views on the length of time sheep spent in the wilderness, but *Bezah*, 40a, suggests that they remained in the open both on hot days and in the rainy season, i.e., all year round. See also *Shekalim*, vii, 4, and Alfred Edersheim, *The Life and Times of Jesus the Messiah* (Eerdmans, 1936), I, 186f. The statement of Stephen A. Haboush is from his letter to the author, January 23, 1971.

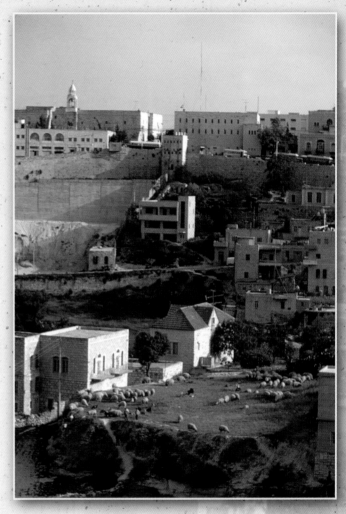

Sheep still graze in a small field below modern Bethlehem. The tower of the Church of the Nativity rises in the top left background.

A Bethlehem Grotto

While they were there, the time came for her to deliver her child. And she gave birth to her firstborn son and wrapped him in bands of cloth, and laid him in a manger, because there was no place for them in the inn.

—LUKE 2:6–7

Some critics doubt that Jesus was born in Bethlehem and argue instead for Nazareth or elsewhere. Such opinions, however, are based only on scholarly conjecture, and no source has been discovered to date that disproves Jesus' birth in Bethlehem.[1]

It is almost certain that Joseph and Mary reached Bethlehem in the late afternoon or early evening. Had they arrived earlier, lodging would not have been so difficult to find, although Bethlehem would have been crowded enough with the many descendants of King David returning to register at their ancestral home.

The picture of Joseph going from door to door, desperately begging shelter because Mary was in labor, has always struck a poignant chord amid the joy wreathing the rest of the Christmas story. And the nameless innkeeper who refused them refuge is usually associated with Judas Iscariot in the popular mind. But probably he—or was it his sympathetic wife?—remembered the cave behind the inn, where animals were sheltered, and he threw it open to the hapless couple. The hills around Bethlehem are perforated with such caverns, and they are still used to shelter cattle and sheep. Grateful for any refuge in the crisis of his wife's birth pangs, Joseph carefully led the donkey and its precious burden down a steep path behind the caravansary to the cave below it.

From all accounts of the Nativity, it seems that no one assisted Mary at the birth of Jesus—not even Joseph, for husbands were not to play the role of midwives. Self-delivery was by no means uncommon at the time. The women of Palestine, unlike

(*Right*) The Church of the Nativity at Bethlehem is the structure in the left half of the photograph. A grotto under the altar of this, the oldest church in Christendom, marks the presumed place where Jesus was born.

The doorway of the Church of the Nativity in Bethlehem is partially walled up, permitting only children to enter without stooping. The Crusaders reduced the size of the entrance to prevent Arab horsemen from galloping into the interior.

Interior of the Church of the Nativity at Bethlehem.

neighboring mothers, prided themselves on delivering their babies rather easily and were quite able to take care of themselves in the absence of a midwife, though physicians and midwives were also regularly used. Luke simply relates that Mary gave birth to her firstborn son, wrapped him in bands of swaddling cloth, and laid him in a feeding trough, which must have had the sweetish, grainy smell of hay, barley, and oats.

And so the incredible paradox happened at Bethlehem: History's greatest figure was born, not in a palace or mansion, but in a cavern-stable. For Joseph and Mary, the holiest moment of all must have come before the shepherds paid their famous visit, as they gazed at the extraordinary baby whose mission even they could scarcely comprehend. Small wonder that this has been the most familiar scene in all the florid history of art. Each generation, each school, has attempted to portray the Nativity, with backgrounds ranging from Oriental to Italian to Flemish, and yet the tableau of the Holy Family in the Bethlehem grotto has remained an unconquered artistic challenge.

There is evidence that someone in Bethlehem relented and offered more normal accommodations to Joseph, Mary, and the newborn Jesus. For, by the time the Wise Men arrived to present their gifts, the Holy Family seems to have been living in a "house" (Matt. 2:11). Or, as happens on any vacation trip today, the motel vacancies that are nonexistent on the night of arrival because the traveler failed to call ahead for reservations quickly materialize the next day.

All Bethlehem must have rustled with news about "that poor girl from Galilee" who had no sooner arrived in town than she bore a child, since the shepherds and, later, the Magi had no trouble finding the Holy Family. Clearly they must have been directed by the townspeople.

Jesus' birth in this particular town had vast implications for the people of Palestine. Bethlehem, which means "House of Bread," was not only the setting for the story of Ruth, but later became the birthplace of David, and here the prophet Samuel anointed him king. Later, it became the expected birthplace of that great "Son of David," or "Messiah," who was supposed to liberate the land from foreign control. It was no accident that over in Jerusalem, King Herod's priests came up with Bethlehem as the logical place to send the Wise Men for any newborn *Christ*, the Greek translation for the Hebrew *Messiah*.2

The Site Today

"O little town of Bethlehem, how still we see thee lie. . . ." The lyrics fit not only the village of the first Christmas but also the town of today. Two millennia seem to have brushed few changes into the Bethlehem scene. It remains a comparatively small town, six miles southwest of Jerusalem, and quiet enough— although the more than thirty thousand who now live there have considerably increased its population from Jesus' day, and confrontations between the Arab population and neighboring Israeli authorities disturb the peace periodically.

Today, the tourist almost always approaches Bethlehem from the north—as Joseph and Mary had done—on a curvy road that twists along a bleak ridge. From a final bend, just outside the city, the so-called Shepherds' Fields are pointed out. This is the presumed place where the herdsmen were watching their flocks at the time of the angelic announcement. The rolling slopes are covered with tawny grasses and dotted with drab scrubby bushes and some pines. Individual fields are fenced off by low stone walls or rows of silver-green olive trees.

Bethlehem itself is a maze of twisting cobblestone lanes, all of which seem to lead into the past. But they find a hub in the centrally located Manger Square, where the crowning sanctuary is the ancient Church of the Nativity, erected by the Byzantine emperor Justinian. This basilica is a less-than-impressive structure of whitish stone that seems to contrast too fiercely with the deep and often cloudless blue sky hanging over the town. A low, partially walled-up doorway compels a visitor to bend down upon entering the sanctuary.

Original mosaic in the floor of the Church of the Nativity, visible today under wooden trapdoors.

Niche in the Grotto of the Nativity, with votive lanterns over the birth site.

43

The Grotto of the Nativity in Bethlehem, marking the traditional site where Jesus was born.

The interior of the church is cool, dark, and hardly imposing, but parts of the nave date back to the time of Constantine, making this Christendom's oldest church in continuous use. Forty-four rose-colored columns with Corinthian capitals divide the nave from its two side aisles, and a round, shiny Christmas tree ornament dangles from each of its lighting fixtures.

From the choir, stairways lead down to a thirteen-by-thirty-three-foot cavern underneath the high altar of the church, known as the Grotto of the Nativity, presumed to be the very cave in which Jesus was born. The place of birth is marked by a low, semicircular niche of white marble surrounding a polished silver star on the floor, illuminated by a collection of overornate lanterns suspended from above. Around the inner hub of the fourteen-pointed star is an inscription: "HIC DE VIRGINE MARIA JESUS CHRISTUS NATUS EST," Latin for "Here Jesus Christ was born of the Virgin Mary." Rich curtains and tapestries adorn the sacred precinct, as well as the little adjacent niche containing a stone manger where, supposedly, the infant Jesus was laid.

Visitors are often struck by conflicting impressions. There is reverence for the holy place, certainly, and some form of Christian worship is usually taking place at the shrine, led by a Coptic, Syriac, Armenian, Greek Orthodox, or Roman Catholic priest. But there is also aesthetic disappointment: the potpourri of garish votive lanterns, icons, and candelabra that cluster about the shrine offend Western tastes. Yet, this is a trifling and parochial objection, for the grotto is, after all, in the hands of Eastern Christendom.

But the dominant question in the mind of any thinking contemporary visitor to the shrine must be this: Did it all really happen here—at this spot? Though final proof is necessarily lacking, the surprising answer lurks closer to *probably* than *possibly*.

Where there is no direct archaeological evidence—and there could be none in the case of the birth of Jesus—nothing is more important in

(Right) A fourteen-pointed silver star in the Grotto of the Nativity marks the presumed place where Jesus was born.

44

establishing the authenticity of an ancient site than antiquity: the place must have been regarded as such from earliest times. If the Church of the Nativity had been built here in A.D. 600, for example, its claims to mark the authentic site of the birth of Jesus would be almost worthless. But Constantine the Great, the first Christian emperor of Rome, erected the original Church of the Nativity at this place in A.D. 326, over the very grotto that had been identified as the true site by the early church father Origen and, before him, Justin Martyr, writing in A.D. 150. Justin stated that Jesus was born in a cave that was used as a stable—not the typical stone or wooden stable so familiar in Christmas art.[3] Earlier still, in the 130s, the pagan Roman emperor Hadrian tried to desecrate the Jewish and Christian holy places in Palestine but, ironically, thereby preserved their identity!

After he had put down an insurrection by the Jewish nationalist and would-be Messiah, Bar-Kokhba, in A.D. 135, Hadrian expelled the Jews from Jerusalem and paganized all known holy places of Jews and Christians, erecting a temple to Venus at the site of the Holy Sepulcher in Jerusalem and a grove dedicated to Adonis over the Grotto of the Nativity in Bethlehem.

After visiting the latter in the early 200s, Origen later wrote: "In Bethlehem the grotto was shown where Jesus was born. . . . What was shown to me is familiar to everyone in the area. The heathen themselves tell anyone willing to listen that in the said grotto a certain Jesus was born whom the Christians revere" (*Contra Celsum*, 1.51).

"How still we see thee lie . . ."

Having hosted the birth of the individual who would change history, Bethlehem seemed content to rest on its laurels, for nothing spectacular has happened there in the two thousand years since. One prominent exception, of course, was the sojourn of Jerome, who lived in the Church of the Nativity complex about A.D. 400 and translated parts

(Left) Votive candles burn just outside the Grotto of the Nativity.

Stone mangers of the type used in Palestine during biblical times have been excavated at Solomon's Stables in Megiddo. Packed with straw, they provided a safe resting place for infants.

THE CHURCH OF THE NATIVITY

FRONTAL FLOOR PLAN AND GROTTO

A. The Grotto of the Nativity.

B. Niche marking the spot where Jesus was born.

C. Site of the manger, where he was laid.

D. Staircases leading from the church down to the Grotto.

E. Subterranean chambers.

F. High altar of the basilica.

G. Columns of the basilica.

of the Old Testament into Latin, which, with other translations, eventually became the famed Vulgate. The Vulgate has remained the official version of the Bible for Roman Catholicism ever since.

And, in the modern era, it was a Syrian-Christian merchant in Bethlehem who first received the original Dead Sea Scrolls from the desert Bedouins who had discovered them in the early spring of 1947. The merchant brought them to the attention of religious authorities in Jerusalem, who alerted the entire scholarly world. Today, Bethlehem turns a brisk trade in religious items—candles, crucifixes, and sacred mementos of olive wood and mother-of-pearl—for the many tourists from all parts of the world who throng the site where Christ was born. The town also bristles with churches representing all principal branches of world Christianity, while the environs of the Judean wilderness are dotted with monasteries, some quite ancient.

Each Christmas, Bethlehem decks itself in colored lights, glass lanterns, glittering stars, and illuminated crosses, while it swells in size because of the influx of Christian pilgrims. On Christmas Eve, a Protestant carol service is conducted at twilight on a hillside at the Shepherds' Fields and again at nine in an outer court of the Church of the Nativity. Meanwhile, the Latin patriarch of Jerusalem leads a colorful procession from the Holy City to Bethlehem in order to conduct a midnight Mass in the Church of the Nativity, a celebration transmitted by closed-circuit television to a large screen in Manger Square for the benefit of the thousands who cannot crowd inside the basilica. At the same time, the Grotto has been filled with humanity for most of Christmas Eve, as groups from all over the world read the Christmas story in a babble of foreign tongues.

Exactly at midnight, a silver bell tinkles in the Grotto, heralding Christ's birthday, and many of the pilgrims are overcome as they spirit themselves back two thousand years and try to find a place between the shepherds at the mangerside. A few move forward to try to press their lips to the metallic star marker. Then church bells peal forth throughout the city since the people of Bethlehem are predominantly Christian.

"The hopes and fears of all the years. . . ."

The end of the first stanza in Phillips Brooks's great Christmas carol, although written in 1868, applies prophetically today, since the "Little Town of Bethlehem" is often torn between serenity and strife. The two thousandth anniversary of Jesus' birth, for example, was supposed to be a glorious bimillennial celebration in the town where he was born, with parades, marching bands, and choirs participating from all over the world. Due to Arab-Israeli hostilities, however, Christmas A.D. 2000 saw Manger Square stripped of its usual holiday decorations and twinkling lights, with only a handful of tourists and pilgrims to observe the milestone.

After the fear, however, the hope returns. Far more often than not, Bethlehem sparkles each December with illumination, celebration, music, and worship—a living Christmas card sent to the entire world.

Endnotes

1. Was Jesus born in Bethlehem? Scholars who doubt this include R. E. Brown, *The Birth of the Messiah* (Garden City: Doubleday, 1977); and M. Grant, *Jesus: An Historian's Review of the Gospels* (New York: Scribner's, 1977).
2. David and Bethlehem: 1 Samuel 17:12ff.; 20:6, 28; 16:1–13. The messianic ruler also was expected to hail from Bethlehem, according to Micah 5:2.
3. Jesus born in a cave: Justin Martyr, *Dialogus* 1xxviii. Justin's reference to a cave as the site is also supported in the *Protevangelium of James* xviii, 1ff.

(*Top*) The Church of the Nativity and (*bottom*) the Manger Square on Christmas Eve. (*A. Lieberman, Israel Government Tourist Office, Chicago*)

Local Shepherds, Distant Magi

In that region there were shepherds living in the fields, keeping watch over their flock by night. Then an angel of the Lord stood before them, and the glory of the Lord shone around them, and they were terrified. But the angel said to them, "Do not be afraid; for see—I am bringing you good news of great joy for all the people: to you is born this day in the city of David a Savior, who is the Messiah, the Lord. This will be a sign for you: you will find a child wrapped in bands of cloth and lying in a manger."

—LUKE 2:8–12

There was something peculiarly public about births in ancient times. There were no hospital maternity wards that only the family could visit, no looking at baby through the nursery window or donning sterile, antiseptic masks. The birth of a baby in Jewish families of the time, especially of a boy, was the signal for general rejoicing in the neighborhood and a feast for the relatives and friends, who came crowding in to see the newborn infant.

But since Joseph and Mary were in special circumstances at Bethlehem, far from their Nazareth home, festivities would be in a different key, even if they did have relatives in the Bethlehem area. Strangely, the only guests at the Nativity mentioned in the New Testament were the shepherds and the Magi.

The Herdsmen

That lowly shepherds should have been the very first to learn about what had happened in Bethlehem has struck some commentators as incongruous, and attempts have been made to "upgrade" the shepherds. So, they are represented as not the ordinary kind of nomadic herdsmen who often infuriated the rabbis by their manner of life, by their sometimes necessary absence from the synagogue, and by their failure to fulfill the Law. Instead, these were supposed to have been special shepherds who were guarding flocks destined for sacrifice in the Jerusalem temple, and this would explain their readiness to welcome a newborn Messiah.[1]

Whether or not this is true, any special "rehabilitation" of the shepherds is hardly necessary in the Nativity account. If, resorting to symbolism, the Wise Men

50

represented privilege, wealth, and intelligence, so the shepherds stood for the cross-sectional, average Judean—quite literally, too, "the man on the night shift." For shepherding was one of the oldest and most important vocations among the ancient Hebrews, who first came into their Promised Land as nomadic shepherds and herdsmen, not as farmers.

The Bible is full of references to sheep and shepherds. Such Old Testament heroes as Abraham, Isaac, Jacob, Moses, and David were all shepherds at some time in their lives, and the Twenty-third Psalm remains one of the most beautiful commentaries on shepherding ever written. In the New Testament, the familiar figure of Jesus as the Good Shepherd underscores the theme. In fact, the modern terms "pastor" and "bishop" both derive from the ancient words for "shepherd" and "overseer-guardian," and to this day the bishop's staff is a shepherd's crook. Perhaps it was highly appropriate, after all, that shepherds be the first guests at the first Christmas.

A modern shepherd at Bethlehem, guarding his flock at night.

They may well have lived in the herdsmen's village of Beit Sahur, just below Bethlehem, and have been pasturing their flocks at night on the sloping expanse just east of Bethlehem that is still pointed out as the Shepherds' Fields. Besides keeping such long hours, herdsmen had to protect their sheep from ravaging animals and robbers by skillful use of staff and sling or a metal-studded club about a yard long. A well-trained sheepdog was almost as effective as the shepherd

An aged shepherd rests at the gate to his pasture in Bethlehem.

in defending the flock. Herdsmen were also expected to shear the wool, aid in lambing, and see that their flocks had enough to eat and drink. While the sheep were grazing, the men often passed the time by playing folk tunes on their pipes.

The names of the shepherds who witnessed the Nativity will doubtless never be known, but they win our respect. Perhaps it was fortunate that they were common laymen, for had they been scholars or theologians, they would likely first have held a debate on the hillside instead of rushing into Bethlehem after the

glad announcement, the conservatives insisting they would never leave the sheep, and the liberals labeling the angelic appearance a mere hallucination. No one has bothered to inquire if anyone stayed behind to watch the sheep while they were gone, but we can safely assume that the first thing the shepherds did the morning after their night of spreading the word about the newborn Christ was to take a head count of their sheep!

The chief breed of sheep in Palestine is the broad-tailed variety (*Ovis laticaudata*), and there is every reason to presume that the flocks still grazing in the hills around Bethlehem today descended from the very sheep whose foraging was so extraordinarily interrupted that night of nights.

The Wise Men

In the time of King Herod, after Jesus was born in Bethlehem of Judea, wise men from the East came to Jerusalem, asking, "Where is the child who has been born king of the Jews? For we

observed his star at its rising, and have come to pay him homage." (Matthew 2:1–2)

How much time elapsed between the adoration of the shepherds and the visit of the Magi is not known, but the mysterious men from the East do not seem to have arrived until after Jesus' presentation at the Temple in Jerusalem, forty days after he was born. Unfortunately, little more is known of the Magi than of the shepherds.

"We three kings of Orient are. . . ." So the beloved Christmas carol begins, but already it has made at least three errors. First, how many Wise Men made the trip to Bethlehem is not known. And they were not "kings." And they did not come from as far away as the "Orient," that is, the Far East.

Tradition, of course, has placed their number at three, probably because of the three gifts of gold, frankincense, and myrrh that they presented to the infant Jesus, the assumption being one gift, one giver. But some earlier traditions make quite a caravan of their visit, setting their number as high as twelve. Legend has also supplied names in the case of the three (Gaspar, Melchior, and Balthasar), and has even reported their ages (twenty, forty, and sixty), as well as their skin colors (white, yellow, and black). But these names arise first in the sixth century A.D., too late for any authenticity, and their ages and races are too obviously spaced.

Supposedly, Thomas, the apostle to India, found and baptized the Magi into the Christian faith, ordaining them as priests. Later, they suffered martyrdom, and their relics were presumably buried in Constantinople but then transferred to the cathedral at Cologne in Germany during the twelfth century, where they rest today. But no one takes such claims seriously.

The Greek of the New Testament calls them simply *magoi apo anatolon*, "magi from the East," and the term *magoi* is usually translated as wise men, astrologers, or magicians. "The East" has been variously identified as any country from Arabia to Media and Persia, but no farther east.

Most of the evidence points to Mesopotamian or Persian origins for the magi, who were an old and powerful priestly caste among both Medes and Persians. These priest-sages, extremely well educated for their day, were specialists in medicine, religion, astronomy, astrology, divination, and magic, and their caste eventually spread across much of the East. As in any other profession, there were both good and bad magi, depending on whether they did research in the sciences or practiced augury, necromancy, and magic. The Persian magi were credited with higher religious and intellectual attainments, while the Babylonian magi were sometimes deemed impostors.

The safest conclusion is that the Magi of Christmas were Persian, for the term originates among the Medo-Persians, and early Syriac traditions give them Persian names. Primitive Christian art in the second-century Roman catacombs dresses them in Persian garments, and a majority of early church fathers interpret them as Persian. Indeed, the reason invading Persians spared the Church of the Nativity in 614

"The Adoration of the Magi" by Albrecht Dürer, painted as altarpiece for the Castle Church in Wittenberg, Germany. Here, baby Jesus playfully tries to grab the golden chest, while a Moorish king stands to the right.

Modes of transportation and dress often seem to have changed little in Palestine during the 2,000 years since Jesus' birth. Here a Bedouin in colorful *keffiyeh*—a versatile insulation against both heat and cold—cajoles his camel.

Sculpture of "The Adoration of the Magi" at the Cathedral of St. Lazarus in Autun, France.

was that they saw a golden mosaic over the doorway, depicting the Wise Men in Persian headdresses.

However, if the astronomical aspects of the Christmas story are emphasized—the great star and its role—a case could be made that the Magi were late Babylonians, since astronomy reached its highest development in Mesopotamia.[2]

Whatever the origin of the Eastern sages, their visit was of great significance for later Christianity: The Wise Men were pagans, not Hebrews, and the fact that Gentile magi performed the same adoration as Jewish shepherds symbolized the universal outreach for future Christianity. "Nations [Gentiles] shall come to your light," the prophet Isaiah had written, "and kings to the brightness of your dawn" (60:3).

The star that guided them to Bethlehem, discussed in the next chapter, had both local and international significance. The Hebrews expected a star as a sign of the birth of the Messiah (Num. 24:17)—a later pseudo-Messiah tried to capitalize on this belief by calling himself Bar-Kokhba, "Son of a Star"[3]—and

Eastern sages were acquainted with Hebrew beliefs because of the large Jewish colony in Babylon and elsewhere. Even Roman authors of the time spoke of the grandiose things expected in Palestine. "There had spread all over the East an old and established belief that it was fated for men coming from Judea at that time to rule the world," wrote Suetonius.[4] Therefore, when the Magi inquired of Herod, "Where is he who has been born king of the Jews?" their question was not really spoken out of a vacuum.

The scene of proud and richly costumed sages worshiping a baby in the humblest of circumstances has etched itself on the world's imagination, for it is a graphic study in contrasts. The gifts they presented are usually interpreted symbolically. Gold, a royal gift, signified Jesus' kingship. Frankincense, a fragrant gum resin burned as incense, denoted his future priesthood. This substance consisted of small whitish beads or chunks that were ground into powder and that gave off an odor like balsam when burned. The third gift, myrrh, called *smyrna* in

Greek, was an aromatic orange-colored resin from the small, thorny trees of the *Commiphora* family. Myrrh was expensive and much esteemed for use in perfumes, anointing oil, medicine, and embalming. That, years later, the crucified Jesus was offered wine mixed with myrrh as a palliative (Mark 15:23) and was also buried with the substance (John 19:39) renders this gift of the Magi predictive enough.

After their adoration at the manger, the Wise Men disappear from history, leaving a multitude of questions in their wake. Almost unidentifiable, they have still become some of the most familiar figures in Western culture, for their clumsy camels have lumbered back into the Nativity scene every year since Christmas was first celebrated.

And they did achieve their purpose in the total story of Christmas, which was to expand it. Up to now, the Nativity had been highly local in nature: only a few people of the lower classes of just one nationality had been involved. But the visit of the Magi burst all that, as rich Gentiles joined poor Jews, as King Herod and the priestly establishment in Jerusalem became concerned, and even the stars looked in.

Endnotes

1. Flocks destined for the temple? Several Old Testament references suggest that the Messiah was expected to be revealed from *Migdal Eder,* "the tower of the flock," near the place where Jacob had buried his wife Rachel (Gen. 35:19–21; Mic. 4:8). Tradition identifies *Migdal-eder* with the shepherd's village of Beit Sahur, near Bethlehem, and the *Mishnah* suggests that flocks pastured there were destined for temple sacrifice. See *Shekalim,* vii, 4, and Edersheim, *Jesus the Messiah,* I, 186f.
2. The Magi: For a full discussion of their origin, see Edwin M. Yamauchi, "The Episode of the Magi," in Vardaman, *Chronos,* 15–39.
3. Bar-Kokhba: Led the Jewish revolt against Rome during the reign of the emperor Hadrian, but was killed by the Romans in A.D. 135. See Dio Cassius 1xix, 12–14; Eusebius, *The Church History* iv, 6.
4. Suetonius on rulers from Judea: *Vespasianus* iv.

The Shepherds' Fields below Bethlehem.

An Extraordinary Star

When they had heard the king, they set out; and there, ahead of them, went the star they had seen at its rising, until it stopped over the place where the child was.

—MATTHEW 2:9

One of the most spectacular aspects of the Christmas story must be the great star that lured the Wise Men from their Eastern homeland to Jerusalem and on again to Bethlehem. For that star never really disappeared. In silver or gold, plastic or cardboard, it crowns the tops of Christmas trees and twinkles among the festive trappings along Main Street. In glitter or aluminum foil, it shines on as the most familiar single motif on Christmas cards.

The Star of Bethlehem has puzzled scholars for centuries. Some have skeptically dismissed the phenomenon as a myth, a mere literary device to call attention to the impor-tance of the Nativity. Some Christians, at the other extreme, have argued that the star was miraculously placed there by God to guide the Magi and is, therefore, beyond all natural explanation. Most authori-ties, however, take a middle course that looks for some astronomical and historical explanation for the Christmas star, and several interest-ing theories have been offered.

First of all, there is nothing in the least improbable about a group of sages being attracted by some astral event and then trying to investigate it more closely. The ancient historians of the Near East, Greece, and Rome were fond of describing astronomical phenomena and the profound effect these had on the daily lives of the people, who were forever interpret-ing their future on the basis of what they saw in the sky each night. In that region of clear air (before any industrial pollution), and in that time of poor artificial lighting, the nights were long and the heavens extraordinarily impressive.

From reading the historical sources, one would think comets, meteors, and other celestial wonders

56

were almost constantly streaking across the ancient skies, and it is no accident that the present mania for astrology is traceable historically to exactly this area of the world. Indeed, the Babylonians first set up the signs of the zodiac.

There is another reason for taking the celestial event in the skies over Palestine quite seriously. If the phenomenon could be identified, astronomy could then also hope to date it, and the mystery of an exact date for the birth of Jesus would be largely solved. Here are the most logical astronomical explanations for the Star of Bethlehem.

Planetary Conjunction

Every 805 years, the planets Jupiter and Saturn come into extraordinary repeated conjunction, with Mars joining the configuration a year later. Since the great Kepler first alerted them to it in the early seventeenth century, astronomers have computed that for ten months in 7 B.C., Jupiter and Saturn traveled very close to each other in the night sky and in May, September, and December of that year, they were conjoined. Mars joined this configuration in February of 6 B.C.—a massing of planets that must have been quite spectacular indeed. But more. The astrological interpretations of such a conjunction would have told the Magi much, if, as seems probable, they shared the astrological lore of the area. For Jupiter and Saturn met each other in

The planetary conjunction of Jupiter and Saturn in Pisces (the Fishes) in December of 7 B.C., as extrapolated from Babylonian records. Modern astronomical calculations place this conjunction in approximately the same position, though a few degrees farther west on the ecliptic. This is a representation of the December sky over Judea, looking toward the southwest, but since a photograph is unable to reproduce the greater intensity of light from the larger planets, Jupiter and Saturn were added with enlarged diameters, as in planetariums. The constellations and stars are identified in the inset above.

that sign of the zodiac called *Pisces,* the "Fishes."

In ancient astrology, the giant planet Jupiter was known as the "King's Planet," for it represented the highest god and ruler of the universe: Marduk to the Babylonians, Zeus to the Greeks, Jupiter to the Romans. And the ringed planet Saturn was deemed the shield or defender of Palestine, while the constellation of the Fishes, which was also associated with Syria and Palestine, represented epochal events and crises.[1] So Jupiter encountering Saturn in the sign of the Fishes would have meant that a cosmic ruler or king was to appear in Palestine at a culmination of history. This, at least, may help to explain why the Magi were well enough informed to look for some "King of the Jews" in Palestine. And the time of this rare conjunction in 7 B.C. fits part of the Nativity chronology very well indeed, even if Jesus were born in 5 B.C. King Herod would later order the slaughter of all male infants in Bethlehem "who were two years old or under, according to the time that he had learned from the wise men" (Matt. 2:16). Seven minus two is five.

But there is a significant objection to this theory: the two or three planets would not have come together closely enough to represent one superstar, for they would always have been separated from each other by at least one or two moon diameters. Rather, they would have appeared as a close pair of very bright stars, as in the accompanying illustration, or as a tight triangle. But the triangle would have been so close to the setting sun in February of 6 B.C. that most astronomers doubt if all three planets could have been seen.[2]

Comet

The Greek term for "star" in the gospel account, *aster,* can mean any luminous heavenly body, including a comet, meteor, nova, or planet. Meteors, brief and brilliant slashes across the skies that they are, would seem too transitory for consideration. But nothing impressed the ancient eye so much as a comet, for comets were thought to herald important changes in the state, particularly by the Romans. Historians of the time

reported that a blood-red comet, so bright that it could be seen in the daytime, dominated the skies in the year that Caesar was assassinated, 44 B.C. A comet also preceded the battle of Philippi, where Caesar was avenged. The death of Augustus was signaled by a comet, too, as were other political crises.

Was the Christmas star really a comet? With its brilliant pointing head and long luminous tail, a comet makes a far more startling impression in the night sky than any planetary conjunction. When Halley's comet passed over Palestine in 1910, Jerusalemites reported that it seemed to pass quickly from east to west, growing somewhat diffused, but nearly reappearing in all its grandeur in the west, much as the phenomenon in the Nativity story. But Halley's comet passed over the skies too early (12 B.C.) in its visit at that time to be the Star of Bethlehem, although it undoubtedly aroused the interest of people in the

(Right) Comet Arend-Roland, named for the Belgians who discovered it, as photographed by the Schmidt telescope at Mount Palomar Observatory on May 1, 1957.

Stars sometimes had special significance for the people of Israel. Here, the six-pointed Star of David is carved within a stone balustrade at Capernaum in Galilee.

The five-pointed Star of Solomon near the same place.

Near East to astral events.

It happens that the Chinese have more exact and more complete astronomical records than the Near East, particularly in their tabulations of comets and novas. In 1871, John Williams published his authoritative list of comets derived from Chinese annals.[3] Now, Comet No. 52 on the Williams list may have special significance for the first Christmas. It appeared for some seventy days in March and April of 5 B.C., near the constellation Capricorn, and would have been visible in both the Far and Near East. As each night wore on, of course, the comet would seem to have moved westward across the southern sky. Since the time is also very appropriate, this *could* have been the Wise Men's astral marker.

Nova

A nova is not really a "new" star, as its name implies, but one that suddenly has a tremendous increase in brilliance, due to internal explosion, and no astral event is more spectacular than this. In our local galaxy of the Milky Way, the last supernova (as it is usually termed today) exploded in 1604, so brightly that it could also be seen in daylight. The ancients sometimes confused comets and novas, though the Chinese usually called the latter "comets without a tail."

It is quite fascinating to note that Comet No. 53 on the Williams list (next after the one previously mentioned) is such a tailless comet and could well have been a nova, as Williams admitted. No. 53 appeared in March and April of 4 B.C.—a year after its predecessor—in the area of the constellation Aquila, which also was visible all over the East. Was this, perhaps, the star that reappeared to the Magi once Herod had directed them to Bethlehem (Matt. 2:9)? Probably not. Herod died about April 1 of 4 B.C., and the audience he granted the Magi would have to have taken place months earlier.

The following, then, is a possible astronomical reconstruction of what happened that first Christmas. The remarkable conjunctions of Jupiter and Saturn in 7–6 B.C. alerted the Magi to important developments in Palestine, for the astrological significance closely paralleled what they had learned from Hebrew lore about a star heralding the expected Messiah. The comet of 5 B.C. (Williams No. 52) dramatically underscored this interpretation and sent them on their way.

That the star went before them "until it stopped over the place where the child was" need not imply any sudden visible movements on the part of the astral phenomenon. Because of the rotation of the earth, anything in the night sky appears to move westward as the night progresses, except Polaris and the relatively few stars north of it. And, as people travel, the stars do seem to "move" with them or before them, "stopping" when they stop. So when it reached a zenith in the skies over Bethlehem, the gleaming blue-white star of Christmas would indeed have seemed to stop for the Magi as they reached their destination.

Even the artistic conceptions of the star shedding its rays down on Bethlehem might not be quite so fanciful as one would think. In subtropical latitudes on very clear nights, a faint luminous band similar to the Milky Way is visible on the southwest horizon. This band, called *zodiacal light,* is the reflection of sunlight on meteoric particles concentrated in the plane of the ecliptic, and it appears as a luminous cone shining from the planetary path down to earth at the point where the sun has set. *If* it appeared to the Magi leaving Jerusalem, zodiacal light might have seemed to beam down from the Christmas star to intersect Bethlehem at the southwest. But this is an embellishment to the Christmas story on which the New Testament is silent.

Perhaps this reconstruction of the astral events seems too pat to be true, and additional astronomical evidence may one day disprove it. But at least it is not so fanciful as some of the current theories. Perhaps the most grotesque is that offered by the Russian V. Zaitsev, who claims that the Star of Bethlehem was really a spaceship from a higher civilization carrying cosmonaut Jesus into this world! But beyond any (more serious) debate, astronomy does play an important role in the history of the Nativity.

Endnotes
1. Saturn as star of Israel: Amos 5:26, in which *Sakkuth* and *Kaiwan* are both names for the Babylonian Saturn. See also Tacitus, *Histories* 5, 4.
2. The Star of Bethlehem: For a summary of current scientific explanations, see Finegan, *Biblical Chronology,* 238–48; W. Burke-Gaffney, "Kepler and the Star of Bethlehem," *Journal of the Royal Astronomical Society of Canada,* XXXI (December 1937), 417–25; and Roy K. Marshall, *The Star of Bethlehem* (Univ. of North Carolina: Morehead Planetarium, 1963). The best monograph arguing for planetary conjunction as explanation for the star is Konradin Ferrari d'Occhieppo, *Der Stern der Weisen* (Wien: Verlag Herold, 1969). This astronomer also suggests that zodiacal light might have appeared between Jupiter-Saturn and Bethlehem. See also his "The Star of the Magi and Babylonian Astronomy," in Vardaman, *Chronos,* 41–53.
3. The Williams catalog: John Williams, *Observations of Comets from b.c. 611 to a.d. 1640 Extracted from the Chinese Annals* (London: Strangways and Walden, 1871).

Herod the King

When Herod saw that he had been tricked by the wise men, he was infuriated, and he sent and killed all the [male] children in and around Bethlehem who were two years old or under, according to the time that he had learned from the wise men.

—MATTHEW 2:16

It was only natural for the Magi to assume that a newborn king of the Jews would have entered this world in the royal palace at Jerusalem. But wise as they were, their inquiry before King Herod showed no great tact and even less diplomacy. "Where is the child who has been born king of the Jews?" might have sounded more courteous to the king had it been worded: "Where is the new prince who will one day succeed you?" For Herod's suspicious mind immediately warped the Magi's query into: "Where is the *real* king, you impostor?" At the time, Herod mistrusted everyone and thought himself surrounded by young aspirants all plotting to seize his throne.

Probably his first impulse was to clap the mysterious visitors into irons for asking such a question, but his native shrewdness checked it. He would have to pose interest and ferret out whatever information he could from them in order to kill off a possible rival. Instead, then, he assembled his priests and demanded to know where the Messiah-king was expected to be born. On the basis of an Old Testament prophecy, the scholars were able to pinpoint Bethlehem. "And you, Bethlehem, in the land of Judah, are by no means least among the rulers of Judah; for from you shall come a ruler who is to shepherd my people Israel" (Mic. 5:2; Matt. 2:6).

His eyes crinkling with suspicion, even as his face wore a mask of affability, Herod directed his guests to David's city: "Go and search diligently for the child; and when you have found him, bring me word so that I may also go and pay him homage . . ."

". . . in mockery and then kill him!" Herod's mind completed the thought.

And the Wise Men would have done just that but for the sudden change of plans recorded by Matthew: "Having been warned in a dream not to return to Herod, they left for their own country by another road" (2:12). Probably they headed due east into the Judean badlands, brushing just north of the Qumran wilderness community that would one day give the world the Dead Sea Scrolls. Then they crossed the Jordan River ford just above the head of the Dead Sea and returned to their Eastern homeland.

Herod took that snub with all the rage of the deluded and suspicious old paranoid he had become. Ordering the ruthless massacre of all male babies two years old and under in Bethlehem and its vicinity, he hoped that the infant "king" must certainly have been among the victims. Estimating a town of some 1,500 inhabitants at the time, about a dozen to fifteen male babies would have fallen into this category and been slain, for some doubtless escaped detection. The scene of mothers madly trying to hush their crying infants so as not to be discovered, only to see them snatched out of their arms by Herod's soldiers, thrown to the floor, and run through with swords sends a bristle of shock into the Christmas story so utterly discordant with the rest of it. To anyone with even the slightest knowledge of the Nativity, Herod emerges quite clearly as "the monster of the Christmas story."

So incredibly brutal was this slaughter of the innocents that many scholars have superimposed a great question mark over this part of the Nativity record, suggesting that nothing of the kind ever happened. But such a crime was very much in character for Herod in his last years, when illness and court intrigue had nearly deranged the man. He married ten wives, who spawned a wriggling, ambitious brood of sons that turned the palace into a human can of worms in their scheming to succeed him. Flavius Josephus, the first-century Jewish historian, tells it all in graphic detail.

Herod was so jealous of his favorite wife, Mariamme, that on two occasions he ordered that she be killed if he failed to return from a critical mission. And then he finally killed her anyway, as well as her

Bronze
Obv. Helmet with crest and cheek piece; inscription: ΒΑΣΙΛΕΩΣ ΗΡΩΔΟΥ (King Herod); date and monogram as below.
Rev. Circular shield, surrounded by a wavy line.

Bronze
Obv. Tripod with bowl; in field right, monogram ℞ ; left, date: Ⳑ (year 3); inscription: ΒΑΣΙ-ΛΕΩΣ ΗΡΩΔΟΥ (King Herod).
Rev. Thymiaterium (incense burner) between two palm branches.

Bronze
Obv. Anchor; inscription: ΒΑCΙ ΗΡΩΔ (King Herod).
Rev. Double cornucopia with caduceus between horns.

Bronze coinage of Herod the Great. (*The Interpreter's Dictionary of the Bible,* © Abingdon)

A diagram of Herod's Temple. (*Three's Company, London*)

Within the diagram:
Antonia Tower
Scale: meters
50   100   150
Pool
Court of Gentiles
N
Court of the Israelites
Holy of Holies   Altar   The Beautiful Gate
Court of Women
Golden Gate
Temple sanctuary   Nicanor Gate
Court of the Priests
Balustrade warning Gentiles not to enter the sacred precincts
Court of Gentiles
Royal Portico

grandfather, her mother, his brother-in-law, and three of his sons, not to mention numerous subjects. During a swimming party at Jericho, he also drowned the high priest, who happened to be another of his brothers-in-law. The real villain behind many of these murders was his sister Salome, who was so jealous of Herod's wives that she sowed the seeds of suspicion for years in the Jerusalem palace, concocting monstrous lies about everyone—lies that Herod too easily believed.

Herod the Great

The young Herod, however, had been an exceptionally able ruler, governing Palestine as client-king on behalf of the Roman emperor Augustus. And the House of Herod had the uncanny knack of being able to sniff the airs of Mediterranean politics and make the right decisions. Herod's father had given crucial help to Julius Caesar when he was down in Egypt, cut off from his supplies, and Caesar rewarded him handsomely for that. Herod himself shrewdly advised his friend Mark

Antony to drop Cleopatra and make peace with Rome. (Antony should have followed that advice.) And once Augustus emerged victorious from the civil wars, he was so impressed with young Herod that he allowed him to become one of his most intimate friends.

The face of Palestine was groomed and beautified during Herod's thirty-three-year reign. Across the land he erected palaces, fortresses, temples, aqueducts, cities, and—his crowning achievement—the great new temple in Jerusalem. He created the magnificent port of Caesarea and stimulated trade and commerce. He also patronized culture in Greek cities far from Palestine and easily became the talk of the eastern Mediterranean.

In fallow years or seasons of famine, Herod remitted taxes, and during one crisis he even sold his dinnerware to buy food for the populace. He also served as protector of overseas Jews in the Dispersion by conciliating their Gentile rulers. He

(*Right*) The fortress Herodium, southeast of Bethlehem, which Herod artificially heightened at the expense of a neighboring hill. Somewhere below the recently excavated citadel, Herod himself is buried.

was so highly respected by Rome that he would actually go down in history as "Herod the Great."[1]

But he had little support in his own kingdom. Herod was only a half-Jew and seemed far too romanizing for his subjects, whom he also taxed heavily. Soon he was hated as a tyrant, even by members of his own family. A maddening maze of intrigues infested the palace, and Herod began suspecting every-one, tormented, as he was, by fears of assassination. In his advancing paranoia, he was continually writing to Rome for permission to execute one or two of his own sons for treason. Finally, even his patron and friend Augustus had to admit, "I'd rather be Herod's pig than his son."[2] It was not only a play on the similar-sounding Greek words for *son* and *pig*, but a wry reference to the fact that pork, at least, was not consumed by Jews.

Old and very ill from arterioscle-rosis, Herod worried that no one would mourn his death—a justified concern. So he issued orders from his deathbed that leaders from all parts of Judea were to be locked inside the great hippodrome at Jericho. When he died, archers were to massacre these thousands in cold blood so that there would indeed be universal mourning associated with his death.

This was the Herod at the time of the Nativity. Would he, then, have scrupled at the lives of a few babies in little Bethlehem? Hardly!

As it was, Bethlehem lay just northwest of his favorite fortress-palace, the great breast-shaped mountain called the Herodium, where he was arranging his own tomb. Here, least of all, would he tolerate sedition in the name of any newborn "king of the Jews."

After changing his will three times and attempting suicide, Herod finally contracted a very loathsome disease in the spring of 4 B.C. that ulcerated his digestive system, inflamed his abdomen, rotted his privates, and blocked his breathing. After a last, fevered convulsion, he died.

But alas, Herod's final plans—both of them—miscarried. The Jewish leaders who were jammed inside the hippodrome were not slaughtered but released, on orders of Herod's sister, Salome. And the baby who was supposed to die in the Bethlehem massacre was, instead, in the arms of his mother as she sat astride a donkey en route to refuge in Egypt. That infant, however, was getting used to travel: this was his third trip.

Endnotes
1. Herod: Josephus, *Antiquities* 14:158–17:199; *Jewish War* (hereafter *War*) 1:203–1:669; Matthew 2. See also Paul L. Maier, "Herod and the Infants of Bethlehem" in E. Jerry Vardaman, ed., *Chronos, Kairos, Christos II* (Macon: Mercer University Press, 1998), 169–89.
2. "Herod's pig": Macrobius, *Saturnalia* ii, 4.

(Right) A newly-excavated garden pool in Herod's winter palace at Jericho.

Up to Jerusalem, Down to Egypt

*After eight days had passed, it was
time to circumcise the child; and he
was called Jesus, the name given by
the angel before he was conceived in
the womb. When the time came for
their purification according to the law
of Moses, they brought him up to
Jerusalem to present him to the Lord.*
—LUKE 2:21–22

Travel is as typical of the
modern yuletide as the
blazing Christmas tree itself.
In our mobile society, highways,
railroads, and airlines are crowded
each December as younger members
of the family come home for Christmas and relatives get together for the
holidays. What other society has
nearly made a carol out of "I'll be
Home for Christmas"?

Travel also characterized the first
Christmas. Besides Joseph and
Mary's tedious journey from Galilee
to Bethlehem, there was the im-
mense westward trek of the Wise
Men across hundreds of miles of
desert to Judea and back again. Then,
too, soon after the Nativity, the Holy

Family took three important trips—
two in order to fulfill Jewish religious law and the third to save the
very life of the newborn child.

The Circumcision

On the eighth day after he was
born, every Hebrew boy baby was
circumcised, a token of the special
covenant between God and his
chosen people dating back to
Abraham (Gen. 17:10ff.). At this
ceremony, the child was also formally given his name. The rite
became one of the most important
hallmarks of Judaism, and some of
its savants even claimed that the
higher angels were created in a
circumcised condition!

Under normal circumstances, the
nearest rabbi would have come to
the home of Joseph and Mary to
perform the ceremony, but since they
may still have been living in the
grotto, or more likely in a rented
dwelling at Bethlehem, they probably took the infant to a nearby
synagogue for the all-important rite.
Presumably, Joseph asked the rabbi
to let him help officiate, a common

request in these happy circumstances, and the rabbi easily agreed.

However it happened, the circumcision-naming ceremony was an occasion for great joy among parents, relatives, and friends, with many overtones of the later Christian baptism. In Jesus' case, probably only Joseph, Mary, and the nameless rabbi shared the gladness that another son of Israel had been included in the great covenant with God. And the baby was given a proper scriptural name, that of Moses' successor as leader of the Hebrews: *Joshua* or *Yeshua*. It meant "God saves" or "God is salvation." Later ages would prefer the Greek form of the name, Jesus.

For some days after circumcision, the baby would be uncomfortable, the first token pain and bloodshed in a career that would see considerably more of both.

The Presentation at the Temple

After forty days it was time for Jesus' first longer journey. Moses' law required that women had to purify themselves after childbirth by offer-

"La Circoncisione," a painting by Veneziano in the Louvre, Paris, depicting the Jewish rite prescribed for every Hebrew boy eight days after birth.

ings at the tabernacle (or, later, the temple) forty days after the birth of a boy and eighty after that of a girl. It was a simple, six-mile trip north to Jerusalem, doubtless on the same patient little donkey that had carried Mary down to Bethlehem, and it should not have taken more than two hours.

The magnificent temple in Jerusalem was approaching completion at the time, a gleaming white jewel

wedged into the northeastern corner of the city. The sprawling enclave was rimmed with a labyrinth of colonnaded porticoes and gates, and to all pious Jews this was the very center of the world. What Joseph and Mary offered for her purification showed how poor they were, for in lieu of sacrificing an unblemished yearling lamb, they offered a pair of turtledoves or pigeons (Lev. 12), the minimum requirement of religious law.

At the same time they also formally presented the infant Jesus back to God in fulfillment of Exodus 13:2 ("Consecrate to me all the first-born . . ."), redeeming, or buying him back again, through an offering of five silver shekels (Num. 18:16). This shows, incidentally, that Jesus was free of any bodily blemish, or this ceremony would not have been necessary.

Everything had happened normally enough up to that moment. But then, as Joseph and Mary were

standing with their bundled infant in the Court of the Women at the great temple, a righteous and devout old man named Simeon walked purposefully over to them with a strange glint in his eyes. For years he had been waiting for the fulfillment of messianic expectations, he explained to the awestruck couple, and God had assured him that he would indeed live to see the infant Christ. That very morning he had been inspired to come into the temple and view the culmination of his hopes. Exuberantly taking the baby in his arms, old Simeon exulted:

> *Master, now you are dismissing your servant in peace, according to your word; for my eyes have seen your salvation, which you have prepared in the presence of all peoples, a light for revelation to the Gentiles, and for glory to your people Israel. (Luke 2:29–32)*

The words would ring down in Christian history as one of the most beloved prayers of the church, and

"La Presentation de Jesus au Temple," a painting by Simon Vouet in the Louvre, Paris, showing the ceremony required for Hebrew males forty days after birth.

artists would never tire of trying to catch on canvas the sacred fire in Simeon's eyes.

Then Simeon turned to Joseph and Mary and blessed them, adding some prophetic words: "This child is destined for the falling and the rising of many in Israel, and to be a sign that will be opposed. . . ." And so Simeon had played out his role as a transition figure, the man, more than any other, who stands between the Old and New Testaments, rooted in the ancient scriptural promises and prophecies, yet gazing at their fulfillment.

Old as Simeon looked, his face almost took on the bloom of youth compared with the decrepit figure that now hobbled over to them, her leathery skin mottled with bleached or browned patches and deeply latticed with wrinkles. Her name was Anna, her role was that of prophetess, and she had been a human fixture at the temple for most of her incredible life span. She was either eighty-four or about one hundred and six years old, since Luke's language is not explicit. Anna came from the tribe of Asher—clearly, the so-called "Ten Lost Tribes" of Israel had not lost all their members—and she formed the perfect female counterpart to Simeon, thanking God and immediately telling others of the wonder that had happened in the form of the six-week-old Jesus.

The Flight to Egypt

> Now after they [the wise men] had left, an angel of the Lord appeared to Joseph in a dream and said, "Get up, take the child and his mother, and flee to Egypt, and remain there until I tell you; for Herod is about to search for the child, to destroy him."
> (Matthew 2:13)

Shortly after Joseph and Mary returned to Bethlehem at the close of their astonishing day at the temple, their sense of wonder was only compounded by the visit of the Magi. But the brimming happiness of the first Christmas was abruptly cut short by what was more properly Joseph's nightmare than his dream, alerting him to Herod's designs on Jesus. Without even waiting for the morning light, Joseph roused his sleeping family; packed the drowsy, dumbfounded donkey; and they all set out on the highway south toward Hebron. The journey down to Egypt would be far more ambitious than that which led from Nazareth to Bethlehem—well over twice as long.

The New Testament tells us nothing about the route they took, but the regular caravan trail from Bethlehem led south on the Hebron road, then sharply west to Gaza and the coastal highway down to Pelusium, the portal to Egypt. An alternate route lay in the desert interior, but it would have been extremely dangerous for a lone couple and baby to try to brave the howling sands of the northern Sinai. With an average of twenty miles per day of fairly level travel along the coastal route, the Holy Family would reach Egypt in about ten days.

Wherever the Bible is silent,

(Left) Panorama of Egypt, the Red Sea, the Sinai peninsula, Palestine (upper center), and across the Arabian desert to the Euphrates River valley (extreme upper right), taken by the Gemini II mission with astronauts Conrad and Gordon in September 1966. The dotted line indicates the most likely route taken by the Holy Family on the Flight to Egypt. The arrow at center points to the traditional Mt. Sinai. (NASA) legend is highly vocal. And so the apocryphal *Arabic Gospel of the Infancy* tries to fill in the details of the flight to Egypt. One of its "charming" stories tells how Joseph and Mary were waylaid by robbers on the Sinai road, but they found nothing to steal from the poor couple. Taking pity on them instead, the bandits gave them provisions and sent them on their way. One of these likeable brigands, of course, would cross Jesus' path thirty years later at the Crucifixion. Who but the penitent thief on his right?[1]

Another apocryphal story has a very hungry Mary looking longingly at a date palm tree and wishing that, somehow, she could feast on its fruit. The infant Jesus smiled, and the palm bent down so that Mary could pick its dates![2]

Many kindred Jews, with whom Joseph and Mary could have sought refuge, were living in Egypt at the time. In fact, more Jews lived in Alexandria than in Jerusalem, forming 40 percent of the population there. But it seems unlikely that the Holy Family would have traveled that far west in the Nile delta. Their place of sojourn in Egypt is unknown, although two late traditions have tried to identify it.

Near the ruins of Heliopolis, outside Cairo, pilgrims as early as the fifth century visited the "Tree of Mary," a spreading sycamore under which Mary is supposed to have shaded herself. And in the Coptic quarter of Old Cairo stands the church of St. Sergius, below which is a crypt venerated from the sixth century as the place where the Holy Family stayed for three months while in Egypt. The crypt was originally a cave or grotto, and visitors are still shown a niche in the wall where the baby Jesus is supposed to have slept. Elsewhere in Egypt, more Coptic churches are dedicated to the Virgin or to events surrounding the Nativity than to any other theme.

Wherever they stayed, it could not have been for long, since King Herod died soon after Joseph and Mary had fled from Bethlehem. Matthew finishes his version of the Christmas story by telling of another angelic dream, in which Joseph is alerted to Herod's demise and is told to return to Palestine, fulfilling the prophecy "Out of Egypt I called my son" (Hos. 11:1).

When Joseph and Mary returned to their homeland, an unhappy surprise awaited them. Herod was indeed dead, but his son Archelaus ruled Judea as his successor, and he had begun his reign with a massacre of three thousand Jews who had rebelled against him in the temple at Jerusalem.[3] Better to return home to Galilee, they decided, where a milder son of Herod, named Antipas, had been appointed tetrarch, with the kind permission of the Roman emperor Augustus.

Endnotes

1. The Robber story: *Arabic Gospel of the Infancy*, xxiii. This and other apocryphal writings about Joseph, Mary, and the child Jesus are most conveniently available in text or outline form in Montague R. James, *The Apocryphal New Testament* (Oxford: Clarendon, 1924).
2. Mary and the palm tree: *The Gospel of Pseudo-Matthew* 20f.
3. Archelaus kills 3,000: Josephus, *Antiquities* 17:213ff.

(Right) The great pyramids and sphinx at Gizeh, near Cairo, which had already been standing some 2,500 years by the time the Holy Family reached Egypt.

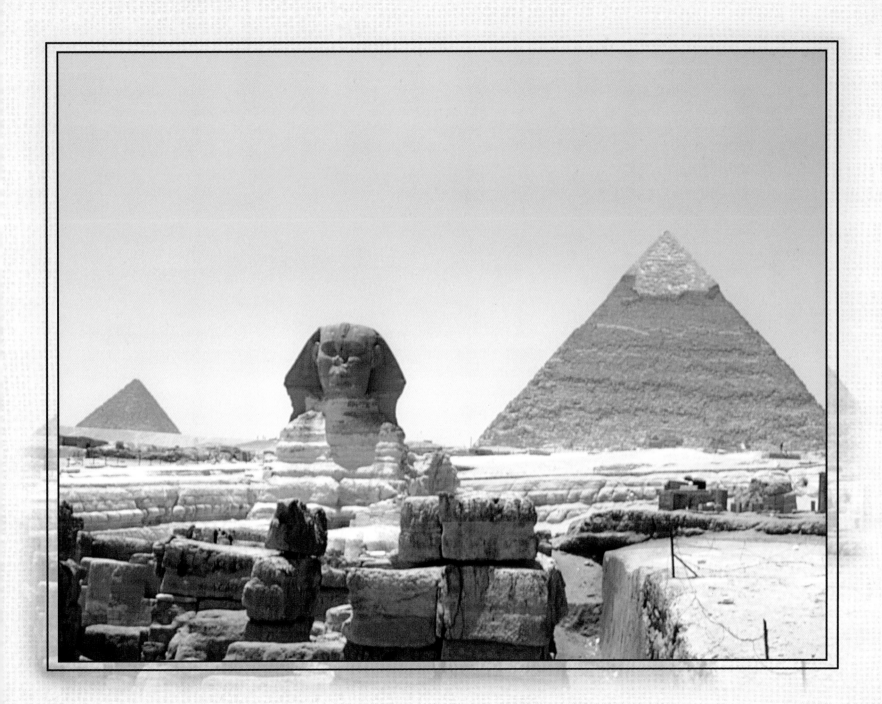

Joseph the Carpenter

"Is not this the carpenter's son? Is not his mother called Mary?"
—MATTHEW 13:55

The focal point of any Nativity scene or of any crèche under the Christmas tree lies just over the heads of the adoring shepherds and Wise Men. It is a husband and wife flanking a manger, looking down on the Child with a magnificent mixture of joy and wonder.

Joseph and Mary would become history's most famous couple because of the all-but-incredible circumstances. Mary was the baby's mother, but Joseph served only as its foster father, according to Christian theology, with God himself the true father. (Liberal theologians, however, and non-Christians generally deny the Virgin Birth.) If Joseph himself harbored any human misgivings about the extraordinary role his wife had been called upon to play, they are not recorded in the New Testament. Nor is there any hint that he chafed at not being able to assert his marital rights before the birth of Jesus, which would have been easy grounds for divorce in the courts today.

There are very few glimpses of Joseph in the Bible, and most of these are tied in with the Christmas story. Here the attractive figure of a considerate, protective, mature individual—a truly good man—playing his difficult role obediently and well is unmistakable. He did not resent the intrusion of shepherds and Magi but rejoiced with them in the birth of a son whom they all believed to be the long-awaited Messiah-king. A pious Jew, he saw to it that the circumcision and presentation of the infant Jesus went according to Old Testament schedule. A good provider and defender, he managed the lengthy trips to and from Egypt with no recorded difficulty—hardly a mean accomplishment for desert travel. By any measure, the noble Joseph is the unsung hero of the Nativity.

The Craftsman

Up in Nazareth, he was known as Joseph the carpenter. And like the famous patriarch Joseph for whom he was named, he, too, seems to have had a father named Jacob, of whom nothing is known save that he was the son of Matthan, and so on up the famous genealogy given at the beginning of Matthew's gospel.[1]

Joseph may also have been born in Bethlehem, since his ancestors lived there, and this is where he came to register for the Roman census. But why, in that case, had he moved up to Nazareth? Perhaps it was economic competition from Bethlehem's too plentiful supply of craftsmen, or it may have been some construction project in Galilee that drew him north. It seems he was not planning to live there permanently, for after the flight to Egypt, Joseph was thinking of returning to Bethlehem. It was only when he learned that Herod's son Archelaus ruled in Judea that he was frightened away from the land and turned back to Nazareth. The Galilean village would take on fresh importance

now, since Sepphoris, which had overshadowed it, had just been destroyed because it had served as headquarters for Judas, a Galilean rebel.[2] Then, too, with most of her family in Galilee, Mary was doubtless just as happy.

After that, the obedient Joseph almost drops out of recorded history. Twelve years later comes a final glance at him in the role of a puzzled parent, wondering what had become of his prodigy-son during a trip to Jerusalem for the Passover festival. At the time, the almost-teenage Jesus was holding theological discussions with savants in the temple, but he quickly returned with his parents to Nazareth and was obedient to them.

After giving Jesus a normal up-bringing, Joseph started training him to be an apprentice carpenter, for later Jesus could even be called a "carpenter" as such. In a revealing passage in Mark's record, the Galileans, amazed at Jesus' teachings, asked, "Where did this man get all this? . . . Is not this the carpenter, the son of Mary?" (6:2–3). The apocryphal *Gospel of Thomas* tells several

Israelite carpenter's tools, discovered in archaeological excavations at Gezer. *(Palestine Exploration Fund)*

Joseph instructs Jesus in the carpenter's trade.

charming stories of Jesus at work in the carpenter shop, miraculously extending the length of several beams that Joseph had not cut to the proper size.[3]

But after this, nothing more is heard of Joseph. At no time does he appear again during the three-year public ministry of Jesus, and the safest assumption is that he had died in the meantime. His wife, Mary, however, emerges at several important incidents in Jesus' career, including the Crucifixion, for which Joseph would certainly have been present had he been alive.

Another important, but overlooked, clue that Joseph did not live to see the culmination of Jesus' career comes from the Christmas record itself. When Joseph and Mary were presenting the infant Christ at the Temple, the aged Simeon turned only to Mary when he prophesied, "And a sword will pierce your own soul too," indicating that the sorrows of Golgotha would affect Mary but not Joseph. Luke, who certainly wrote his gospel after the death of Joseph, saw no reason to adjust that prediction but simply related it (2:35).

Again, however, tradition and legend have exuberantly sketched in the areas left blank by the New Testament. The *Protevangelium of James* and the *History of Joseph the Carpenter*, both apocryphal works of the second and fourth centuries respectively, portray Joseph as a widower with children when he became engaged to Mary, who was presumably only twelve years old at the time. Joseph himself worked in the timber yards of Galilee, according to these sources, and also made tabernacles along the Sea of Galilee. Supposedly, he died at the ripe old age of 111.[4] Needless to say these traditions have little value.

Other Children?

But this does raise the question of whether or not Joseph and Mary had children after the birth of Jesus and were an otherwise normal family. The evidence is much disputed. Several passages in the New Testament seem to provide an obvious

(Right) A view across Nazareth, where Jesus spent his youth. The dark conical structure at the left center is the dome of the Church of the Annunciation.

answer, for they do indeed mention brothers and sisters of Jesus. For example, here is the full reaction of the Galileans at the start of Jesus' public ministry: "Is not this the carpenter, the son of Mary and brother of James and Joses and Judas and Simon, and are not his sisters here with us?" (Mark 6:3). The identical listing is repeated in Matthew 13:55, with the exception of "Joseph" for "Joses." The names of the sisters are not given anywhere in the New Testament, though the apocryphal *History of Joseph* calls them Assia and Lydia.[5]

The Protestant interpretation, generally, is to take the passages at face value and reply: Yes, Jesus did indeed have half-brothers and half-sisters, and these are their names, at least in the case of the men. Matthew's statement that Joseph engaged in no marital privileges with Mary "until she had borne a son"

(1:25) is often cited to support this interpretation, as is Luke's assertion that she gave birth to "her firstborn son" (2:7).

At first, these brothers were indifferent to, or critical of, Jesus (John 7:5), but after the Crucifixion, they became active Christians and leaders of the early church (Acts 1:14). James became the first bishop of the Christian church in Jerusalem, and Judas presumably wrote the letter of Jude in the New Testament.

Nevertheless, Roman Catholicism, Eastern Orthodoxy, and some Protestants affirm the perpetual virginity of Mary and identify the brothers and sisters either as children of Joseph by a prior marriage or as Jesus' cousins, the children of Mary, wife of Alphaeus, who was the sister of the Virgin Mary. The term "brother" is usually used in the New Testament in the literal sense but sometimes may indicate cousins, close relatives, and friends.

Christendom has lived very comfortably with either interpretation, even while theologians continue to debate the issue. The New Testament has the happy habit of

being a little less than explicit in areas that do not pertain to the core of the faith.

Endnotes

1. The father of Joseph: Given as Jacob, son of Matthan, in Matthew's genealogy (1:15f.), but as Heli, son of Matthat, in Luke's account (3:23f.). The two genealogies are different back to David, after which they are identical back to Abraham. The differences in the genealogies are explained in chapter 3.
2. Destruction of Sepphoris: Josephus, *Antiquities* 17:289.
3. Jesus extends Joseph's beam: *Gospel of Thomas* (Greek A) xiii.
4. Joseph dies at 111: *History of Joseph the Carpenter* x, xvff.
5. Sisters of Jesus: *History of Joseph the Carpenter* ii.

(*Left*) "Finding of the Savior in the Temple" by Holman Hunt. Joseph, at the upper right, shows satisfaction at locating the twelve-year-old Jesus in the Temple at Jerusalem. (*Birmingham Museums, Birmingham, England*)

Mary the Virgin

And Mary said, "My soul magnifies the Lord, and my spirit rejoices in God my Savior, for he has looked with favor on the lowliness of his servant."

—LUKE 1:46–48

Whether or not she had other children after Jesus, Mary occupies a wholly unique place in the history of religion. All three major branches of Christianity—Roman Catholicism, Protestantism, and Eastern Orthodoxy—agree with Mary's own prediction in the Magnificat. Because of her extraordinary role in bearing Jesus, she said, "from now on all generations will call me blessed" (Luke 1:48). And they have done just that, in painting, carving, sculpture, hymnody, verse, prose, prayer, and whatever other media can communicate human feeling.

It was a simple Galilean girl who made so apparently extravagant a prediction. Critics may claim that the author of the third gospel put the words into her mouth, but even if that were true the statement continues to amaze, since these words were first written down about A.D. 65–70, at a time when the tiny Christian church was undergoing what seemed a bloody and terminal persecution. And yet, Mary is recorded as saying that all future generations would know of her role in the Christmas event, which is exactly what happened *in fact!*

The little fifteen- or sixteen-year-old Jewess was called by an alternate form of the name of Moses' sister Miriam. *Mary* meant, approximately, "the Lord's beloved," and it was as common in Palestine at the time as it is today. She was undoubtedly of Davidic descent, while a very early tradition identifies her parents as Joachim and Anna.

This source, the *Protevangelium of James,* is an apocryphal work of the second century A.D. that was the first to sketch in so many of the details missing in the pre-Christmas story about Mary. It tells of the pious Joachim and Anna, who had been married for many years, but without any offspring—a humiliating sorrow for them both. The wealthy old couple prayed so fervently for a child that an angel finally announced to each separately that they would have a daughter.[1]

After Mary was born, so the *Protevangelium* continues, Joachim and Anna gratefully dedicated her when she was only three years old to a life of service at the temple. Little Mary eagerly skipped up the fifteen steps at the gate of the temple and, without so much as a backward glance at her parents, she remained there until she was twelve years old "like a dove that dwelt there, and she received food from the hand of an angel."[2]

Later, she and six other virgins were given the task of weaving a new scarlet and purple curtain for the temple, and it was while she was engaged in this work that the angelic Annunciation took place. But when her pregnancy was discovered, Mary and her elderly protector-betrothed Joseph were brought before the high priest, protesting their innocence. Both were forced to undergo the water test for adultery, which would have caused a miscarriage, according to Old Testament law (Num. 5:16ff.). But they passed the ordeal successfully.

Finally, the apocryphon has its own version of the events in Bethlehem. It tells of Joseph searching for a midwife while Mary took shelter in a cave. As the midwife approached the cavern with Joseph, a great cloud obscured it and then an intense light appeared. The clouds broke to reveal the newborn infant, nursing at Mary's breast.

These may be charming additions to the Christmas story, but are they reliable or historical? While so early a source as the second-century *Protevangelium* must command a good deal of respect, the document was proscribed as heretical by the very earliest papal *Index,* and its embellishments, however picturesque, are not accepted as authentic today.

The Sites in Nazareth

Sometimes archaeology can supply hard evidence in place of the

"Madonna and Child" sculpture over the tomb of Raphael in the Pantheon at Rome.

Across the centuries, the "Madonna and Child" motif has been sentimentalized, as in this saccharine example. (The violin will not be invented until 1500 years later.)

flimsies of literary fantasy, and efforts have been made to locate Mary's childhood home in Nazareth, as well as the house she later shared with Joseph and Jesus. But the results are much disputed.

Today, to be sure, visitors are shown the Church of the Annunciation, the largest Christian sanctuary in the Near East, constructed over the rockhewn Grotto of the Annunciation, where Mary presumably lived and was greeted by the angel. Eloquent Latin words still identify the mystery of the Incarnation in metal lettering over the base of the altar erected there: "VERBUM CARO HIC FACTUM EST"—"Here the Word was Made Flesh."

Some distance north of the Church of the Annunciation stands the Church of St. Joseph, so named because it is commonly believed to shelter in its crypt Mary and Joseph's house and workshop, the place where Jesus spent his boyhood. And west of the church is a chapel supposedly built over the synagogue where Jesus gave his first public address in his hometown (Luke 4:16ff.). Even the fountain or well where Mary drew her water has been marked by an adjacent chapel, the Church of St. Gabriel, where Eastern Orthodoxy believes the Annunciation took place. The *Protevangelium of James* has Mary accosted for the first time by the angel as she drew water here.[3]

But are these sites authentic? Unfortunately, the identifications are rather precarious because the task of locating the true sites has been severely complicated by the fact that Christian shrines were not erected here until well into the fourth century A.D., and they were later devastated by Muslim attacks. Since there is only one natural spring in Nazareth, however, the "Well of Mary" may be authentic, and water seems to have been drawn from it for two millennia and more. Today, Nazareth is the largest Christian city in Israel and also contains its largest Arab population.

Mary's Later Life

Unlike Joseph, Mary appears at several important episodes in her son's public ministry, and her

84

various vignettes in the New Testament show a woman of much spiritual sensitivity, loyalty, and concern, even at times when she, like the disciples, did not seem to understand the fathomless depths of Jesus' mission. Yet, even at his crucifixion she stood as the grieving but submissive model of all that was finest in Jewish motherhood, as Jesus commended her into the care of his disciple John.

After the New Testament accounts of Christ's death and resurrection, a new fulfillment brightened Mary's life as she finally plumbed the whole dimension of Jesus' renewed existence, and she was closely associated with the disciples in the founding of the Jerusalem church. From this point on, history breaks off, and various early traditions have Mary accompanying John to Asia Minor or remaining in Judea. One record tells of her spending the rest of her days in Ephesus and finally dying there, while another

The "Madonna and Child" motif was a favorite in the Renaissance. Raphael painted this so-called "Large Cowper Madonna" at Rome in 1508. (*National Gallery of Art, Washington*)

"The Madonna Before Arched Walls," painted by Albrecht Dürer. (*Capuchin Monestary, Bagnacavallo, Italy*)

legend has her death and assumption in Jerusalem, as witnessed by the apostles, who had been miraculously reassembled.[4]

Because of her absolutely unique role in bearing the man whom Christians call the Son of God, two thousand years of theology would further explore Mary's role, culminating in 1854, when Roman Catholicism officially defined her as both sinless and immaculately conceived, and in 1950, when it declared her bodily assumption into heaven. Protestants, however, deny these dogmas because of the lack of New Testament evidence.

The most familiar view of Mary, however, is the Mary of Christmas, rejoicing not only in the natural experience of motherhood but in reverent awe at the extraordinary son she had brought into the world. There would be sorrow ahead—not just the rigorous journey into Egypt but the future fact of Calvary. Yet, for the present, Mary would rejoice.

And she also had enough presence of mind to serve as historian for the exceptional event in the absence of any historians: "But Mary treasured all these words and pondered them in her heart" (Luke 2:19). This reflective attitude also characterizes Mary after the episode of the twelve-year-old Jesus in the temple (Luke 2:51). According to earliest church tradition, it was Mary herself who told Matthew and Luke all about the Nativity, and it was they who wrote it down. And that is how we got the story of the first Christmas.

Endnotes

1. The father of Mary: Given as Joachim in Christian tradition (*Protevangelium of James* i, 1ff.). The name Heli (see previous note on the father of Joseph) is the diminutive of Eliachim, which is an alternate form of Joachim. Therefore, some scholars consider Luke's genealogy that of Mary herself and the name of her father in the *Protevangelium* substantiated. However, no definite name for Mary's father or mother is given in the New Testament.
2. "Like a dove": *Protevangelium* viii, 1.
3. Annunciation at the well in Nazareth: "And she [Mary] took a pitcher and went forth to fill it with water. And behold, a voice said, 'Hail, thou that art highly favored, the Lord is with thee . . .'" (*Protevangelium* xi, 1). But this apocryphon has the angel complete the Annunciation back in her home as she wove the temple veil.
4. Apocryphal versions of Mary's death: Coptic and Syriac texts, as well as Greek and Latin narratives grouped under the title "The Passing of Mary," especially the *Transitus Sanctae Mariae.*

(*Right*) "Here the Word was made flesh"—the Latin lettering reads—in a crypt below the altar in the Church of the Annunciation in Nazareth.

Jesus of Nazareth

They returned to Galilee, to their own town of Nazareth. The child grew and became strong, filled with wisdom; and the favor of God was upon him.

—LUKE 2:39-40

The baby is what it was all about. If he had not grown up to become the Jesus Christ of the New Testament, we would never even have heard of the story of Christmas, despite its beauty, simplicity, and wonder. But something began at the Nativity that has never ended. The infant would change history, wrench the world's chronology so that its years would pivot about his birth, and touch countries, cultures, civilizations, and untold millions of lives.

Whenever those strange public-opinion polls are taken, asking, "Who is the most admired man in history?" Jesus of Nazareth has no trouble vastly outdistancing everyone else. However the child of Christmas is regarded—Son of God or mortal man—there is no question that his life affected the future more than that of any other human being who ever lived. For the Christianity that he founded has become the most successful single phenomenon in the history of the world: no other religion, philosophy, way of life, nation, or cause has commanded the loyalties of two billion people—in the present generation alone—and none is so widespread.

The supreme paradox must be this: The person behind this achievement taught publicly for only three and one-half years. He wrote no book. He had no powerful religious or political machine behind him—indeed, the ranking spiritual and governmental authorities opposed him—and yet he became the central figure in human history.

The book about him now has billions of copies in print in a thousand languages, and yet no one even wrote his biography in our sense of the term, since the four accounts of him given in the Gospels offer detail only on the two extremities of his life:

his birth and his last three years. Two of the Gospels are silent on his birth, and of the some thirty intervening years, we know next to nothing. The only reported episode happened when Joseph and Mary took the twelve-year-old Jesus along with them to Jerusalem for their annual Passover festival visit, but then lost him in the Holy City. Their astonishment at finding the lad sitting among the scholars in the temple, amazing them by his intellectual expertise, is as familiar as the Nativity itself.[1]

The Hidden Years

The Gospels were never intended as full biographies in the modern sense but rather as records of Jesus' public ministry. They focus, then, not on the thirty "hidden years," as they are called, when he grew to manhood and prepared his mission, but on the all-important forty-two months after he came out of obscurity. Only then was he finally old enough to be listened to by his countrymen, who never really trusted anyone *under* thirty in matters religious.

But Jesus was also a human being—and humans love childhood stories—so, once again, the apocryphal gospels were only too happy to supply them. Several of the anecdotes are pleasant enough. When he was a three-year-old toddler, Jesus took a dried fish, put it in a basin of water, and ordered it to shed its salt and come back to life. The fish, of course, did just that, swimming happily about.[2] Several years later, Jesus was out playing with some neighborhood boys, and he made twelve model sparrows out of clay. When he clapped his hands, the birds came to life, and they flew away chirping.[3] Then there was the time two great snakes slithered out of a cave, sending his playmates running off screaming. But Jesus calmly ordered the creatures to prostrate themselves at Mary's feet, which they promptly did.

He had no trouble getting down from precarious perches. Once, while he was playing on a roof in Nazareth—obviously Mary was not around at the time—Jesus simply grabbed onto a shaft of sunlight and slid down on it to the ground. Other

A fresco from the Catacomb of Sts. Marcellinus and Peter showing the woman with hemorrhages touching Jesus' cloak in seeking a cure (Mark 5:25ff.). Eusebius reports that she came from Caesarea Philippi.

stories tell of his healing people long before his teens and even raising one of his chums, named Zeno, from the dead.

But the other apocryphal childhood tales are not so charming. In one of them, Jesus was acting like a precocious "brat" in school, not only rattling off the alphabet far in advance of his classmates but proceeding to explain the architecture behind each letter. When the schoolmaster tried to slap him, he found his own hand withering instead.[4] In some of the stories, Jesus appears as an almighty urchin—a dangerous enough combination—with no control over his cruel and childish caprice. So one of his playmates, who accidentally hit Jesus in the shoulder, fell over dead when Jesus cursed him, and the parents of the stricken child begged Joseph to take Jesus away "or at least teach him to bless and not to curse." When Joseph reprimanded Jesus and twisted his ear, the lad warned, "I am *not* yours. Don't vex me!"[5]

Another playmate, who offended Jesus less, was merely changed into a ram. And vice versa: once, when Jesus rode a mule, the animal was released from some magical curse and turned back into a fine young man.

Needless to say, each of these puerile stories has as much validity as a fairy tale and as much substance as a fantasy. One wonders why medieval artists were so impressed with them as themes for their canvas and stained glass. The fourth gospel is clear in suggesting that Jesus' first miracle did not take place until he was an adult, at the Galilean marriage in Cana (John 2:11).

An Apprentice Carpenter

These may have become years of silence for subsequent ages, but they were normal enough for the child Jesus. Some missing pieces of the picture-puzzle of his youth can easily be carved to fit. His schooling, for example, was probably no different from that of the other village children in Nazareth. His first lessons inevitably came from Mary. But when he was about five, Jesus, like other Jewish children of the time, received much of his primary educa-

90

tion at the synagogue, where he and the other pupils sat on the floor about the *hassan*, or teacher, repeating verses from the Torah until they knew them by heart. Jesus could read and write both Aramaic and Hebrew, and he undoubtedly knew common Greek as well, for he seems to have had no trouble conversing with the Syrophoenician woman or with Pontius Pilate. A few Latin words are sprinkled in his vocabulary as well.[6]

He also had to learn a trade of some kind, for it was a rule among the Jews that every man had to work with his hands, even those destined for a religious profession. "Whoever fails to teach his son a craft teaches him to steal" was a rabbinical maxim. The great Rabbi Hillel was a woodcutter, the later apostle Paul of Tarsus a tentmaker, and Jesus of Nazareth a carpenter, like his foster father. In Jesus' case there was probably the added necessity of learning a craft to supplement the family's meager income.

The early church father, Justin Martyr, born in Samaria around A.D. 100, wrote that Joseph and Jesus specialized in plows and yokes in their carpenter shop. They were of excellent, durable quality, Justin claimed, and some of them were still in use in the mid-second century.[7]

Carpenters of the time also constructed beds, boxes, coffins, benches, stools, troughs, and threshing boards, as well as more elaborate projects like boats and houses. Though the first floors of nearly all homes in Nazareth would be cut out of the soft limestone of the hill in which the town is situated, or built of stone blocks, the upper stories of larger houses were made of wood. The bronze and iron tools the carpenters used have been found in excavations at Galilee and elsewhere, and some of them have a familiar, almost modern, design. Only the power tools, it seems, are missing. And wooden joints were mitered, mortised, or dovetailed in the same configurations learned in any high school shop classes today.

There were also specialist carpenters who did inlay work and even carved artificial teeth. Skilled carpentry was late in arriving in Palestine, for David had to import Tyrian carpenters to build his palace and

Each Christmas, these bells in the tower of the Church of the Nativity at Bethlehem peal forth at midnight to announce the festival.

Solomon his temple, while Ezra had to bring in Phoenician craftsmen even to repair it.

Images at Maturity

One old tradition, the *History of Joseph the Carpenter,* has Jesus a nineteen-year-old when Joseph died. This is very possible. In that case, if Joseph had married between the ages of twenty-five and thirty, he would have died when he was nearly fifty, which was about the average life expectancy for the time, though many lived longer.

Jesus was now a man—a man who has been the subject of more books, treatises, studies, and tracts than any other person in history. But, apart from the many familiar accounts of his extraordinary ministry, what was he really like?

His physical appearance is not certain. Because of the famous Hebrew restriction against idolatry— "You shall not make for yourself a graven image, or any likeness of anything" (Exod. 20:4 RSV)—art suffered among the Jews, and the earliest representations of Jesus are not Jewish but Roman. In the Christian catacombs, he is pictured as a beardless Roman youth tending sheep, though in fact he probably wore a trimmed beard in the style of his fellow Galileans.

The earliest bronze statue of Jesus could well have been authentic, for the church historian Eusebius himself saw it in the Gentile city of Caesarea Philippi near the base of Mt. Hermon. It was said to have been erected by the woman whom Jesus had healed of a chronic hemorrhage (Mark 5:25ff.), and it showed her resting on one knee in the position of a suppliant before the figure of Christ, who wore "a double cloak neatly draped over his shoulders with his hand stretched out to the woman." But this statue was destroyed by the emperor Julian "the Apostate."[8] Luke, a Gentile Greek, is supposed to have painted likenesses of Jesus, Peter, and Paul, but no trace of these has been found.

Jesus' physical appearance must have seemed very normal indeed— no towering figure, no nimbus, no halo. His enemies required the services of a Judas to point him out in the dusk of Jerusalem, Mary Magdalene mistook him for a gardener at the Easter tomb, and to the Emmaus disciples he looked like nothing more than a fellow traveler.

Yet he must have been an arresting figure of great intellect and much oratorical ability—persuasive, attractive, impressive. Crowds could listen to him for hours, since he spoke with authority. To his enemies, however, he appeared as a deceiver, a blasphemer, a false prophet. The response to Jesus, then, was hardly ever neutral. He captured the people or antagonized them.

He was no ascetic: he enjoyed a good time, provided party supplies on one famous occasion, and loved good friendships and people at every level, especially children. He was no legalist: if someone needed healing on the Sabbath, he simply healed. He was not intolerant: he ate with hated publicans and obvious sinners. Nor was Jesus the namby-pamby, soft-and-sweet sort of person conjured up in so much art: he had an athletic vigor that could enable him to stay up all night in prayer or

The Changing Face of Jesus. In the early church, he was portrayed as a youthful "Good Shepherd," as in this fourth-century sculpture, following Luke 15:4–5. (*Pio Christian Museum, Rome*)

A thirteenth-century Byzantine mosaic in Hagia Sophia basilica, Constantinople (Istanbul, Turkey), shows the transcendent Christ.

Rembrandt's portrait shows a Christ of both humility and majesty. (*Metropolitan Museum of Art, New York*) single-handedly drive the money changers out of the temple with a whip. He was a man totally committed to his mission of announcing the kingdom of God and then dying to make it all possible.

Even though future ages would enthrone him as the greatest individual who ever lived and Christians acclaim him as the God-man, Jesus always had a sensitivity for the past, and he was continually quoting the Old Testament. One very luminous part of that past he could never forget, since Mary must have told him the story again and again, as mothers will. And even Jesus must have marveled at it, because he was so human: the story of angels over Bethlehem . . . the story of adoring shepherds and humbled Wise Men . . . the story of the first Christmas.

Endnotes

1. Temple visit at age twelve: Luke 2:41–52.
2. Jesus and the fish: *Gospel of Thomas* (Latin) i.
3. Jesus and the birds: *Gospel of Thomas* (Greek A) ii.
4. Jesus at school: *Arabic Gospel of the Infancy* xlviii–xlix.
5. Jesus supposedly curses a child: *Gospel of Thomas* (Greek A) iv–v. The other childhood stories derive from this and other apocryphal infancy narratives.
6. Jesus' linguistic abilities: Luke 4:17ff.; John 8:6–8. Mark 7:26ff. tells of the meeting with the Syrophoenician woman. The Latin terms in his recorded speech include *modius* (Matt. 5:15); *quadrans* (Matt. 5:26); *legio* (Matt. 26:53).
7. Plows made by Jesus: Justin Martyr, *Dialogus* lxxxviii.
8. Bronze statue of Jesus: Eusebius, *The Church History* vii, 18.

(*Right*) The Temple Mount in Jerusalem, now the site of the Islamic shrine, the Dome of the Rock, constructed in A.D. 691. The Mount of Olives looms in the background.

List of Photographs, Maps, and Illustrations